Books and Monographs
by William C. Byham

Understanding job analysis—with P. Hauenstein

Applying a systems approach to personnel activities

Three thrusts toward cultural change (Practical suggestions for turning vision into reality)

The assessment center method and methodology: New applications and technologies

Assessment centers and managerial performance—with G. C. Thornton III

Dimensions of managerial competence: What they are, how they differ between levels, how they are changing (rev. ed.)

Targeted Feedback: Making subjective data objective

Review of legal cases and opinions dealing with assessment centers and content validity (rev. ed.)

Applying the assessment center method—with J. L. Moses, eds.

Changing employee behavior—with D. Bobin, eds.

Four-day work week—with J. A. Wilson, eds.

Confrontation with change: Women in the work force—with M. Katzell, eds.

Alternatives to paper-and-pencil testing—with D. Bobin, eds.

Women: Action not reaction—with D. Slevin, eds.

The law and personnel testing—with M. E. Spitzer

The uses of personnel research

Zapp!

The Lightning of Empowerment

How to improve productivity, quality, and employee satisfaction

William C. Byham, Ph.D.
with Jeff Cox

**Harmony
Books
New York**

Published by Harmony Books, 201 East 50th Street, New York, New York 10022. Member of the Crown Publishing Group. Originally published by Development Dimensions International Publications.

Harmony and colophon are trademarks of Crown Publishers, Inc.

Manufactured in the United States of America

Library of Congress Cataloging-in-Publication Data
Byham, William C.
    Zapp! : the lightning of empowerment / William Byham.
      p.   cm.
    1. Communication in management. 2. Interpersonal relations.
    I. Title
    HD30.3.B94   1991
    650.1'3—dc20   90-41460
                                         CIP

ISBN 0-517-58283-X
10 9 8 7 6 5 4 3 2 1

First Harmony Books Edition

Preface

Why Should You Read This Book?

That's a fair question. Why *should* a serious, rational adult in business today take time to read a fable about the troubles and triumphs of workers in a make-believe department headed by a guy named Joe Mode? Frankly, your own career is one good reason for reading *Zapp!* The success and survival of the organization you work for is another.

To do business in the markets of the late 20th Century, in a global economy, and often against excellent competitors, it is essential to keep working for constant improvement, for what the Japanese call *kaizen.* This means that in a world-class organization, everybody in the company has to be thinking every day about ways to make the business better in quality, output, costs, sales, and customer satisfaction. In government and other public service organizations as well as in business, there are demands for higher performance.

More and more in years to come, the successful organizations will be the ones best able to apply the creative energy of individuals toward constant improvement. Yet, constant improvement is a value that cannot be imposed upon people. It has to come from the individual. The only way to get people to adopt constant improvement as a way of life in doing daily business is by *empowering* them.

That is what *Zapp!* is about. It deals with the basic principles of empowering people, about helping employees take ownership of their jobs so that they take personal interest in improving the performance of the organization. This book can help you understand on a fundamental, practical level what empowerment really is, why it is important, and how to start using its key principles on the job.

v

Why did we write the book in the style of a fable? Because even the best ideas are of small value unless communicated well. *Zapp!* is written the way it is so that we could take an abstract concept and let people visualize it in action, and in lively but meaningful terms. We wanted the book to be easy to understand, but challenging to the imagination.

There are two ways to read the book. Most people will find the story amusing and will probably finish this book in one or two sittings. But if you're in a hurry, skim through the sections called "Joe Mode's Notebook." These summarize the essence of the book and outline the basic principles of empowerment. The better way, however, is to read the story, which lets you discover the ideas, and try to deduce the conclusions as you go along.

Fable or not, this is a realistic, practical book. We expect that after you have read *Zapp!*, you will have the knowledge to start putting the underlying ideas to work, and a basis for beginning formal training in empowerment skills and related areas. So we hope you enjoy *Zapp!*, and, more important, that you learn about what has become a concept vital to personal and organizational success.

WILLIAM C. BYHAM, Pittsburgh, Pennsylvania

Part I

Situation Normal

1

Once upon a time, in a magic land called America, there lived a normal guy named Ralph Rosco.

Ralph worked in Dept N of the Normal Company in Normalburg, USA. For years, Normal had been a leading manufacturer of normalators, those amazing devices which are so fundamental to society as we know it.

As you might expect, just about everything was normal at Normal, including the understanding of who was normally supposed to do what:

Managers did the thinking.

Supervisors did the talking.

And employees did the doing.

That was the way it had always been—ever since Norman Normal had invented the normalator and founded the company—and so everybody just assumed that was the way it should always be.

Ralph was your normal type of employee. He came to work. He did the jobs his supervisor told him to do. And at the end of the day he dragged himself home to get ready to do it all again.

When friends or family asked him how he liked his work, Ralph would say, "Oh, it's all right, I guess. Not very exciting, but I guess that's normal. Anyway, it's a job and the pay is OK."

In truth, working for the Normal Company was not very satisfying for Ralph, though he was not sure why. The pay was more than OK; it was good. The benefits were fine. The working conditions were safe. Yet something seemed to be missing.

But Ralph figured there wasn't much he could do to change things at Normal. After all, he reasoned, who would even bother to listen? So at work he kept his thoughts to himself, and just did what he was told.

Ralph worked on a subsystem of what was technically termed "the guts" of the Normal normalator. One day on his way back from lunch, Ralph happened to be thinking about the guts of the normalator, and—well, he was simply ZAPPED by an idea so original and so full of promise that his head nearly exploded with excitement.

"Wowee! Zowee!! Yeah!!!" exclaimed Ralph—to the shock of the Normal employees around him.

In his excitement, Ralph totally forgot that probably nobody would listen, and he ran down the hall to explain his idea to his supervisor, Joe Mode.

Ralph found Joe Mode busy doing what he normally did. He was telling everybody what to do as he worried about each of the 167 rush jobs that had to be done by the end of the day as he added some figures while he scribbled a memo in the middle of taking an urgent call from *his* boss, Mary Ellen Krabofski.

"Mode, I want you to start cracking the whip down there," Krabofski was telling him.

"But I do crack the whip," Joe said. "Every chance I get."

"Well, whatever you're doing, it's not good enough. All the big bosses are pacing in their offices. They say the competition is stiff and getting stiffer. Sales are low and getting lower. Profits are thin and getting thinner. So you'd better do something quick, or else!"

"But what can I do?" Joe asked in desperation.

"Raise that productivity, Mode! Cut those costs! Boost that quality! And, above all, do not let your efficiencies slip!"

"Right, got it," said Joe.

"Then get to it!"

And they both hung up. That was when Joe saw Ralph standing off to the side eagerly waiting to talk about his idea.

"So talk," said Mode.

Ralph explained his idea, which was so original and full of promise, as Joe continued doing everything he was already doing.

"But that isn't what I gave you to work on," said

Joe. "How are you coming with that rush job you're supposed to have done by the end of the day?"

"OK, I'll finish it. But what about my idea?" asked Ralph.

"It doesn't sound to me like the Normal way to do things," said Joe. "And don't you think if that idea is good, the Normal R&D people would have thought of it?

"But, tell you what, when I get time I'll kick it upstairs and we'll see what happens. Maybe they'll form a task force to look into it."

At that moment, Ralph was tempted to tell Joe that he didn't want his idea to be kicked anywhere by anybody, and that *furthermore . . .*

But being normal, Ralph didn't tell Joe anything. He just nodded, and went back to work—and Joe went back to telling everybody what to do and worrying about the 167 rush jobs that had to get done.

By the end of the day, Ralph somehow had managed not to finish the job Joe needed. He left it and bolted for the parking lot with the others. And Joe, with a sense of defeat, sat down at his desk and worried about Mary Ellen Krabofski.

2

One thing to Joe Mode's credit, he was organized. Over the years, he had developed the habit of writing things down, and all this jotting and scribbling had evolved into a notebook he kept. Sitting there at his desk, Joe got out his notebook and wrote down the problem as he saw it.

Joe Mode's Notebook

The problem as I see it:

- My boss wants more . . .

- Because management needs more . . .

- Because the customers demand more . . .

- Because competitors are delivering more.

But I can't get my people to *do* more than the bare minimum.

Then he wrote down all the symptoms of what he thought might be wrong.

Joe Mode's Notebook

What is wrong:

- Hardly anybody gets excited about anything that has to do with work.

- The things they do get excited about are outside of work.

- My people care about their paychecks, their vacations, and their pensions. Beyond that, forget it.

- The general attitude is: Don't do anything you don't have to do. Then do as little as possible.

Notebook (cont'd)

- All day, it's like everybody is in slow motion—until it's time to go home. Then it's like watching a videotape in fast forward.

- I talk about doing a better job and what happens? Lots of blank looks.

- Nobody takes any more responsibility than they have to. If the jobs don't get done, it's my problem, not theirs.

- Everybody just does enough to get by so they won't get yelled at or get fired.

- Nobody cares about improvements; they're all afraid of change. (Me, too, if I'm honest about it.)

- I say, "If you don't shape up you won't have jobs." But all that does is demoralize them, which makes it worse.

- Whenever I try to motivate people, the results (if any) are short-lived.

Of course, not all of that was absolutely true, and Joe Mode knew there were individual differences between people, but overall that was how it seemed to him.

Then he started a new page, the page where he would come up with a brilliant solution that would solve the entire problem quickly and easily.

He sat there.

And sat there.

And sat there some more.

But no brilliant solution was forthcoming. Finally he wrote . . .

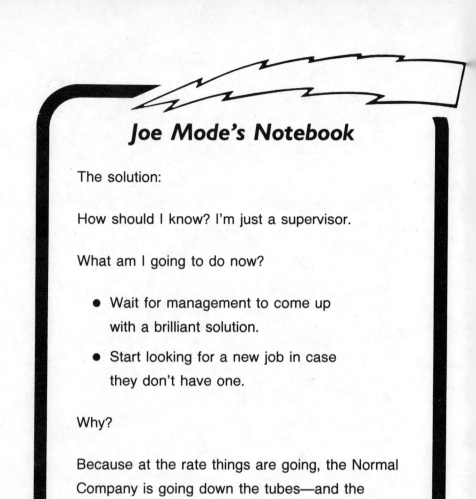

Joe Mode's Notebook

The solution:

How should I know? I'm just a supervisor.

What am I going to do now?

- Wait for management to come up with a brilliant solution.
- Start looking for a new job in case they don't have one.

Why?

Because at the rate things are going, the Normal Company is going down the tubes—and the normalator industry of America won't be far behind!

Then he closed his notebook, locked it away in his desk, and headed home. It had not been a good day.

3

Of course, Joe Mode soon forgot about Ralph's idea. But Ralph did not. And, because of that, something very *ab*normal began to take place.

It so happened that Ralph worked by himself in a remote part of Dept N, a place where Mode normally did not venture very often because it was out of the way.

This allowed Ralph to take many an open-eyed nap on dull afternoons, myopically staring into "the guts" of the normalator until he heard footsteps around the corner, when he would snap into his *normal* work pace.

But after he'd come up with his idea, Ralph found he was actually thinking too much to take naps. He started making little sketches. Then he even started developing his idea using a broken normalator sitting discarded in the corner.

Because no one would understand, he told no one about what he was doing. He sneaked supplies he needed, pilfered the trash bins for scrapped parts he could use, deviated left and right from standard procedures.

Weeks passed. But, little by little, from the old normalator evolved a new device, one that Ralph proudly called:

The Ralpholator

He worked on it whenever he had the chance—odd moments, coffee breaks, during lunchtime. He began coming in earlier and earlier each day so he would have time in the morning to work on it. He even worked faster on the jobs Joe Mode gave him, finishing most of them early so he would have more time for the Ralpholator.

People noticed a change in Ralph. He seemed to have more energy. He seemed younger somehow. He seemed *with it*. He even seemed *happy*.

Of course, Ralph encountered many setbacks and made a multitude of mistakes. But he stuck with it. Finally one morning when Ralph came to work early, he was able to solder the last wires into the control panel, and the Ralpholator was finished.

Naturally, Ralph just had to try it out. He connected the wire leads to his chair, sat down, flipped a few switches, and typed a command on his desktop computer.

A high-pitched whine began to emanate from the innards of the strange machine. His work area began to pulsate with an unearthly light. Ralph gripped the arms of his chair, grinned with anticipation—and vanished in a powerful flash.

A few hours later, Joe Mode needed to know something about a job Ralph was doing and he told his assistant, Phyllis, to go get Ralph. But Ralph was not around.

Grumbling at the inability of corporations to hire good help these days, Joe stomped down the hall, entered Ralph's work area, and was astounded at the tangle of wires running everywhere.

"What's all this?" he rumbled.

He sat down in Ralph's chair, and in doing so, his elbow hit the return key on the computer keyboard. There was a high-pitched whine, a blinding flash of light, and Joe Mode was zapped into the 12th Dimension.

4

Of course, Joe did not know he was in the 12th Dimension. But he knew something had happened. Because, looking around, he saw things were different.

For instance, purple fog was drifting across the floor.

"This is not normal," thought Joe.

And little crinkly lightning bolts were flitting here and there all around Ralph's work area.

"No, this is definitely not normal," thought Joe.

And from the contraption to which all the wires ran there came a strange pinkish glow.

"This is so un-normal, I'm leaving!" thought Joe.

So Joe backed away. He tiptoed through the purple fog, found the exit, and stepped out into the hall, hoping that everything would be normal again. But everything was not. In fact, everything was even more strange.

The fog was thicker and colored in unrelenting shades of gray. Ceilings and corners were shadowy and dark. As Joe was pondering the perplexity of this, the hall was filled with a ghastly green light and from around the corner came a big, scaly troll. Joe began to back away as the troll stomped toward him. Then he noticed something remarkable. Its claws had fingernail polish.

Fire engine-red fingernail polish. Yes, it was exactly the shade always worn by . . .

Joe looked up into the face of the troll and saw that it was the face of his own boss—Mary Ellen Krabofski! She was carrying printouts of the monthly reports under one greenish arm, and she walked right past Joe without even seeing him.

Keeping his distance, he followed her through the fog as she headed straight for Joe's office—and straight up to a faint ice-blue blur, which turned out to be Phyllis.

"Where's Joe Mode?" asked Mary Ellen, her tail twitching.

Phyllis, whose desk was surrounded by sandbags, dove for cover against the expected incoming barrage.

"Mr. Mode is out," muttered Phyllis.

"Well, when he gets back," said Mary Ellen, as one of the computer printouts she was holding curled up into a large black ball and sprouted a smoldering fuse, "you give him this."

And she tossed the black ball over the sandbags to Phyllis and left, a pool of ghastly green leaving with her.

Phyllis quickly took the black ball and its sputtering fuse into Joe's office to leave on his desk.

Joe looked around. How dull and gray it was here. "Where are the fluorescent lights?" he wondered.

But all the normal people were here. He saw them working away in the fog, though he did have a little trouble knowing who some of them were.

A dim ember in the shadows turned out to be good old Mrs. Estello, there in her normal chair pecking away at a computer keyboard—mindlessly making error after error without a break.

"Excuse me," said Joe. "Aren't you going to correct those mistakes?"

But Mrs. Estello's fingers did not even pause.

Next to her, Joe saw another of his workers, Dan, sitting in the dark with both hands tied to the arms of his chair.

A whitish form came shuffling out of the fog and revealed itself as a man wrapped in mummy tape, who in turn revealed himself as Marty, another of Joe's workers.

"Hey, Marty," said Joe. "What's happened here?"

But Marty kept on shuffling, and passed Becky as she went about her work, her eyes burning like candles as she moved like the living dead.

What was it with everybody? They seemed jailed in

dullness, veiled and dim. Joe had to walk right up to them even to see who they were.

And there were walls everywhere. Stone walls, glass walls, steel walls. Everyone had a wall around him. It was like wandering about in a maze.

"What's happened to everybody? Why doesn't anybody talk to me?!" cried Joe in frustration.

"Because they can't see or hear you," said a voice behind him.

Joe turned and found Ralph.

"Ralph! What the heck is going on?" asked Joe. "Is this some kind of dream, nightmare, or what?"

"None of the above," Ralph said. "We're both in the 12th Dimension."

And he and Joe sat down while Ralph explained about the Ralpholator.

"But why is everything so different here?" Joe asked.

"It's not different," said Ralph. "We're just seeing things we can't see in the normal world."

"Yeah? Like what?"

"Like how people feel, what's going on in their minds, what it's like for them on the inside," said Ralph.

"Come on! These can't be the people in *my* department," said Joe. "We only have happy and content employees at the Normal Company—especially in Dept N! Take me back to the real world."

Normally, Ralph would have been intimidated by

Joe Mode and kept his mouth shut. But here in the 12th Dimension, where he had discovered far more than his boss, he was emboldened to look Joe in the eye, shake his head, and say, "You just don't get it, do you?"

"Get what?"

"Look around. Joe, this *is* the real world," said Ralph. "It's the same place, but we're seeing it in a different way. Did you notice that most of the light around here comes from people?"

"Now that you mention it . . ."

"Take Mrs. Estello. Her light is so dim it doesn't even make it to her fingertips," said Ralph. "On the other hand, Mary Ellen Krabofski has a lot more, but her light doesn't shine very far beyond herself, does it?"

"So?" asked Joe.

"I think we're seeing an invisible power that people have—invisible in the normal world, but visible in the 12th Dimension," said Ralph.

"Well, that's very interesting," said Joe. "But let's get out of here and go back to work. If the rest of the 12th Dimension is this gloomy, whatever you're talking about isn't worth bothering with."

"But every place isn't like this!" said Ralph. "Some are even darker and gloomier!"

"Oh, terrific."

"But wait—some are brighter, even brilliant. And

there is one place you have to see before we go back."

"Well, I'd love to, but . . ."

"Really, I insist," said Ralph.

So Joe, realizing that Ralph was pretty much in the driver's seat here, said, "Oh, OK, show me."

And they went off together through the fog.

5

*I*t seemed to Joe that they journeyed a great distance, though in fact it was not very far at all. By and by, the fog thinned and they walked out of the gloom into brightness.

As Joe looked around, he discovered they were in a fascinating place.

Walls here gave structure, but did not confine. And this place did not feel stationary; it felt as if it were in motion.

Most astounding here were the people. They radiated a mysterious energy that lit up the place. Some were brighter than others, but the collective brilliance of all of them was like a small, warm sun.

They did many things. Some worked alone. Some worked together in groups. Yet the light seemed to join them all, flowing from one to the next, connecting them in common purpose.

"There she is!" said Ralph. "Watch that woman over there!"

He pointed to a small, robust woman in a cone-shaped wizard hat who was wandering about.

"Why is she so special?" asked Joe.

"You'll see," said Ralph.

Just then, a door swung open. A young man staggered out. The suit of armor he wore was battered and scorched. His helmet plumes were burned to cinders. His sword was chipped and cracked. Behind him, through the door, Joe and Ralph could see a dragon panting fire.

The woman in the wizard hat went to the man's side. She was talking to him when, suddenly, there appeared in her hand a bolt of lightning.

It forked and flickered and flashed as she held it.

Then, with a graceful windup, she pitched the lightning straight at the young man.

"ZAPP!" went the lightning through the air. And right into the man.

Joe flinched, fearful that the young man would now be dead on the floor. But, on the contrary, he instantly became more alive and glowed brightly.

One by one, the dents in his armor popped out. The scorch marks vanished. New plumes popped out of his helmet as the charred cinders of the old ones fell off. His sword became whole again. And he marched back through the door to face the dragon again.

The door shut behind him. And there were roars and shrieks, clangs of metal, blasts of fire, and all kinds of other noises.

The woman quietly moved on.

She went to the next door along the hall—a brand new one that still had a "wet paint" sign on it. She opened it and, on the other side, a narrow path on a spine of solid rock meandered out to meet the yawning emptiness of a bottomless chasm. Some vast distance across the chasm, the path began again; it zigged and zagged up through many barren cliffs to a mountain encrusted with diamonds.

But there was no way to cross the chasm.

The woman in the wizard hat put her hand on her chin. Then she called to half a dozen people around the hall, and they all came together beside the doorway.

A new huge bolt of lightning forked and flickered and flashed in the woman's hand. As the woman began to talk to them, ZAPP! went the lightning, branching out to every person in the group. And each of them glowed brighter than before.

Then the woman left them, and they went through the new door, out onto the narrow spine of rock together, the glow of the lightning going with them.

They looked around and talked among themselves,

little flickers of their lightning passing among them. Then they set to work.

Some of them built a fire while the others went off and came back with some cloth, rope, and other materials. Two of them began weaving a huge basket, and some of the others started cutting the cloth and sewing it together into an enormous sack. Still others began knotting the rope to make a big net. And pretty soon, it became clear they were building a hot-air balloon to fly themselves across the chasm to the diamonds on the other side.

"Well, I'll be . . ." said Joe.

"I thought you'd be impressed," said Ralph.

"Say, Ralph, what do you think it all means?"

"This is one of the other departments in the company," said Ralph. "I don't know which one, but they sure must have their act together."

Next they noticed a woman answering a phone call. Little by little, she began to glow with lightning. After she hung up, they saw her put two fingers to her mouth and blow a shrill whistle. With a clatter of hooves, a silver horse came prancing over to her.

Suddenly the William Tell Overture (a.k.a., the "Lone Ranger" theme) began to play. The woman got up on the silver horse and took the reins.

"Charge!" she yelled and rode off, the music fading as it followed her down the hall.

Meanwhile, the noises coming from the dragon lair

had slowly diminished. The door opened again. Out came the young man.

His armor was battered again and his plumes were singed. But, this time, the dragon followed him— meekly. On a leash. And everyone realized that he had not only fought the dragon, he had tamed it.

6

*B*oth Joe Mode and Ralph Rosco were fascinated by this incredible sight of human lightning flashing between people and everyone working away at these amazing tasks here in—well, wherever this was.

Meanwhile, Mary Ellen Krabofski, fuming at the inability of corporations to hire good supervisors these days, was furiously searching Dept N for Joe Mode so she could yell at him about the monthly report.

She went stomping into Ralph's work area and tripped over an extension cord, which yanked the plug out of the wall and sent her reeling headfirst into the Ralpholator.

The room went dim, the Ralpholator went dead, and Mary Ellen Krabofski went limp on the floor.

All of a sudden Joe and Ralph began to feel funny. For a few seconds they were not solid anymore. And before their eyes, the lightning zapping between the people dissolved into invisibility.

The young man's armor became a normal shirt and pants.

The dragon became a computer diskette.

The wizard became a rather ordinary woman.

The bottomless chasm became just a plain table with a bunch of people sitting around it.

And the diamond mountain was nowhere to be seen.

Joe and Ralph had materialized in the middle of a normal office with cubicles and desks and chairs. In panic, they were looking for someplace to hide, when the rather ordinary woman turned and saw them.

She wore a name tag, which said:

NORMAL COMPANY

**Lucy Storm
Supervisor-Dept Z**

Surprised to see these two strange men bumping into each other as they attempted to get away before being noticed, she asked, "May I help you two with something?"

"No, thanks," Joe said sheepishly.

"Just passing through," said Ralph.

"Are you lost?" she asked.

Joe and Ralph did not know what to say.

"This is Dept Z," Lucy explained. "We don't get many people passing through down here."

"Oh, well, actually, Ralph here is new to Normal, and I was just showing him around," lied Joe Mode.

"Why didn't you say so," said Lucy Storm with a smile. "Come on. We'll give you the 50-cent tour."

She took them down the aisle and each person they met along the way proudly explained part of what Dept Z did, which sounded so tedious and boring that soon both Joe and Ralph felt their eyes glaze over.

Yet nobody seemed bored here. It looked just like every other office. And yet there was something different in the air. The people here were so *involved* in what they were doing—whatever it was.

Just walking along, Joe and Ralph could not see the lightning, but they could sense that it was there. People moved with purpose. They worked with purpose. They talked with purpose. There was a quiet hustle and bustle throughout the place.

"This is Frank," Lucy said, pointing out a young man holding a computer diskette, who in the 12th Dimension had worn armor. Frank told them a little bit about what he did (which again sounded very dull to Joe and Ralph), then Lucy said:

"Frank found a *dragon* of a problem in our computer system. And he not only found the problem, he kept trying one thing after another to fix it. He thought it had him beat this morning, but we talked for a while and he went back and kept trying until he found the solution. We're all very proud of him."

And just then the woman who had ridden off on the silver horse came through the doors.

"Here comes Emily," said Lucy Storm. "One of our customers called in with an emergency need for a spare part, and even though it isn't really her job, Emily took it on herself to get that part, drive it to the airport, and put it on a plane so the customer can get it this afternoon."

They could almost hear the Lone Ranger theme playing again.

Then they came to the table where some people were working together.

Not wanting to interrupt them, Lucy said, "And this is a team we've put together to develop a new service. If we can just get ourselves to the market, we think it'll be a real diamond mine for us."

"Aha," thought Joe. "They're tackling everyday problems. But it's more than routine; it has more meaning to them. It's all so *personally* important to them."

"You really have something special going on here in your department," Ralph said to Lucy.

"Well, we have a lean staff, but our output meets demand, our customer ratings are great, and our quality is excellent and keeps getting better," Lucy Storm said. "I'd say we must be doing a few things right."

By now, Joe Mode was feeling more than a slight twinge of envy. What was it that made *her* department so good? Did she have some kind of advantage nobody else had?

"You must have your pick of excellent employees to do as well as you have," said Joe.

"No, I've just worked with what Personnel has sent me," said Lucy.

"Then you must have better equipment than everybody else," said Joe.

"Look around," said Lucy. "It's the same computers and telephones every other department has."

"Better systems then," said Joe.

"I wish we did," said Lucy. "But we're stuck with the same systems and policies as everybody else in the company."

"Then what *are* you doing that makes this department so good?" asked Joe.

"Well, it's only partly what I do. It's what we *all* do," she said.

"I know what it is!" exclaimed Ralph. "It's the lightning—!"

For this, Ralph got Joe's elbow poked in his ribs.

"The *what?*" asked Lucy.

"Nothing," said Joe. "He just means that everybody seems so *energized* around here."

"Oh," said Lucy. "Well, I do think everyone feels

good about working here. And I do my best to keep them charged up."

"And just how do you do that?" asked Joe Mode, leaning forward.

"I'd like to think it's just being a good supervisor," she said.

This reply did not satisfy Joe Mode, but by now they were at the door. The complimentary tour was over. They thanked Lucy Storm and headed back home to Dept N.

7

Dept N was operating normally when Joe and Ralph returned.

"Is it quitting time yet?" someone was asking. "Another two hours!? I'll never make it!"

Someone else was saying, "Who cares. Ship it. Let those jerks in the field worry about it."

Up the aisle a third voice was saying, "Hey, slow down! You make the rest of us look bad."

And over in the corner, "They don't pay us to fix things. Call maintenance and take a break."

"But maintenance can't be here until tomorrow."

"So? It's not your problem."

Then everybody saw the boss was back and the whole place went silent.

At this point, however, Ralph was feeling pretty good. His invention was finished and it had worked. He knew he had discovered something important—a whole new way of seeing the world. And he had shown it to his boss, and his boss had seemed impressed. "Things are going to work out just fine," Ralph thought to himself.

But it was not to be.

Back in Ralph's work area, Mary Ellen Krabofski was just getting up off the floor. Her yelling began the moment she laid eyes on them.

What was this stupid contraption she had reeled into? Had the management committee approved of this? What kind of supervisor was Joe Mode for allowing unauthorized projects in his department? Didn't Ralph know that the extension cord she had tripped over was a safety violation? And on and on.

In the end, Ralph got the worst of it. He was forbidden to work on his crazy device ever again. In fact, he was ordered to dismantle it before the end of the day. Then he was given a three-day suspension from work.

Ralph grimly did as he was told.

And Joe headed for his office, passing Phyllis, who was on the phone saying, "Spare part? How should I know? Oh, all right, all right. I'll transfer you to somebody else—oops."

Joe looked at Phyllis and Phyllis looked at Joe.

"I guess they got disconnected," said Phyllis. "Oh well."

"Nope, no lightning here," thought Joe Mode.

He went into his office and sat down at his desk. As soon as he looked at it, Joe felt like that monthly printout from Mary Ellen had exploded in his face.

But the day had not been a waste. Because Joe Mode had seen lightning. Human lightning. He had seen the Zapp!

8

Joe Mode started to wonder.

How come he ran a department where people only cared about quitting time while Lucy Storm ran a department where people really cared about making things better and better?

How come he kept getting yelled at by his boss for not being good enough while she, even with a lean staff, could deliver great performance?

How come?

What was it down there in Dept Z that had made those people so *turned on* about their work?

What was Lucy Storm doing that he was not?

Well, whatever it was, she had the kind of department Joe wanted to run.

Surely it had something to do with the lightning Zapping between the people. What was that lightning? What made it work?

Then Joe realized, "Hmmm, this could be it, the answer to my problems."

Joe got out his notebook.

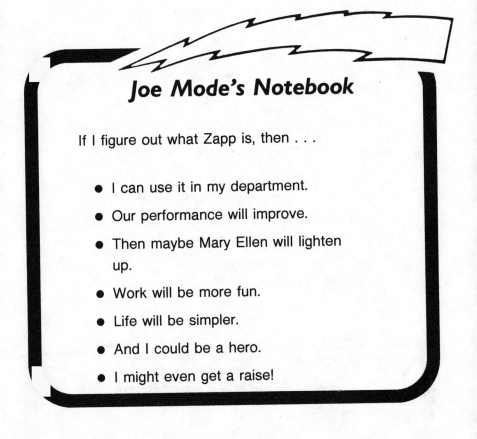

Joe Mode's Notebook

If I figure out what Zapp is, then . . .

- I can use it in my department.
- Our performance will improve.
- Then maybe Mary Ellen will lighten up.
- Work will be more fun.
- Life will be simpler.
- And I could be a hero.
- I might even get a raise!

"And if *she* can do it, *I* can do it!" said Joe.

But how?

Of course, the easy thing to do would have been to

go to Lucy Storm, talk to her directly and openly, and try to learn from her.

Nah! Joe Mode entertained that possibility for only the briefest of split seconds. That would have violated Joe Mode's Three Ironclad Rules:

1. Never ask for help.
2. Never let it seem like you can't handle everything on your own.
3. And never ever talk to anyone about anything important unless you don't have any other choice.

Besides, if he could do this on his own, he might be able to grab all the credit for it. So Joe Mode decided he would figure this out by himself. The first thing he did was give the lightning a name.

He called it Zapp.

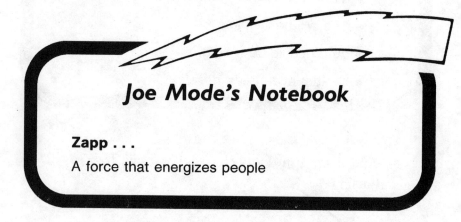

Joe Mode's Notebook

Zapp . . .

A force that energizes people

Now, how could he generate Zapp in Dept N? The problem was you couldn't see Zapp, but it was there. Kind of like excitement—and enthusiasm. Then he remembered that in Dept Z everybody seemed enthusiastic.

"Aha!" said Joe Mode. "She must give them pep talks."

The next day, Joe called everyone together and tried giving them a pep talk.

But nothing much happened. A few people were enthusiastic for about five minutes, then everybody went back to being the way they had been before.

Joe did some more thinking. "Hmmm. Lucy seemed like she was nice to everybody," he thought. "So I'll try being a nice guy for a while."

But that didn't do much either. Most people were nice in return, but nobody did a better job or was more committed to their work as a result.

"Well, no more Mr. Nice Guy," thought Joe Mode. "If being nice didn't make lightning, I'll be Mr. MEAN!"

But being Mr. Mean was no more effective than being Mr. Nice Guy, and sometimes it made things worse. People would jump when Joe appeared, just to slack off when he turned his back. Tensions ran high. Quality plummeted. Union grievances soared.

Not only that, but after Joe did some checking

around, he learned it was extremely rare for Lucy Storm ever to raise her voice to anyone. Yet her people applied themselves to their work, got things done on time, and accepted responsibility.

What could he try next?

Then Joe said, "Hey, I'll bet Zapp is nothing more than one of those quality circles programs!"

He looked into it and indeed Dept Z did have a quality circles program. But then so did Dept Q and Dept B and Dept K—and Joe knew they performed no better than his own Dept N.

Years ago, even Dept N had had its own quality circle. But it had been a big disappointment and, like most of those programs, had soon faded away.

So quality circles were not the same as Zapp.

"I know! Money! Money always talks!" thought Joe. "Those people in Storm's department must get some kind of special bonuses or incentives."

But he did some checking around and learned that Dept Z abided by Normal's normal pay plans, which of course meant no special incentives.

He also found that a few departments *had* tried bonuses and incentives, but had got mixed results. The extra money was always welcomed by those getting it, but often did not do very much except increase costs.

By now, Joe was out of guesses. So he went to Normal's company library, and on one of the dusty shelves he came across a book that mentioned something called "participative management."

It said:

Whatever happened to participative management?

Participative management stems from the idea of involving employees in the decision-making process. The basic idea has been around for a long time, but it's had its ups and downs in terms of popularity.

One of the big problems is that hardly anybody understood what it really meant. In the Fifties, managers thought it meant being friendly to employees. In the Sixties, they thought it meant being sensitive to the needs and motivations of people. In the Seventies, managers thought it meant asking employees for help. In the Eighties, it meant having lots of group meetings.

Using it, different managers would get different results. One manager would call a meeting, and try to get people involved—and it would work. Another manager would do the same thing and nothing would happen.

The very name "participative management" seemed to imply that it was something *management* did (which in turn seemed to limit the degree to which employees would or could participate). Actually, "employee involvement" is a term that goes hand in hand with participative management, and the two terms might almost be used interchangeably.

While participative management has not been a

failure, confusion over what it is (and is not) has prevented widespread success.

Could Dept Z be using participative management? Joe didn't know. He was too confused.

Then Joe read something about job enrichment programs, quality of work life programs, and various other kinds of programs. But Dept Z didn't even have any of those.

Maybe it had to do with the way the company was organized.

The entire Normal Company had gone through a *re*organization last year that had removed some layers of middle management. The top managers had called it "flattening the organization" in the company newspaper and it was supposed to be a good thing.

Joe wasn't so sure. Right after the flattening, *he* had nearly been flattened by the weight of new responsibilities dropped on him. It seemed to Joe that if there were good things about a flattened organization, only Dept Z seemed to know about them.

Then he remembered the group of people sitting around the table in Dept Z—the team!

"That's it!" said Joe. "Work teams!"

But, no, lots of other departments had tried putting people into work teams. Dept Z still had *something* they did not.

And then Joe thought about things like suggestion systems, more training, better communications, a closer labor-management relationship, job security, and lots of others.

In every case, if Dept Z had them, they worked. If other Normal departments had them, they didn't seem to matter much.

Now Joe was really stumped. Nearly all the ideas he'd considered were, he had to admit, very good ones. So he made a list.

Joe Mode's Notebook

Departments have tried:

- Pep talks
- Quality circles
- Higher pay
- Participative management
- Job enrichment
- Quality of work life
- Flattened organization
- Work teams
- Suggestion systems
- More training
- Better communications
- Closer labor-management relationship
- Job security
- And lots of other programs

What happened?

- Results were usually mixed, shortlived, disappointing, counterproductive, confusing, or insignificant—in most Normal departments.
- They only work well when Dept Z tries them.

Now what did that mean?

"That Dept Z has the *key* to making all these other new ideas and programs work, something we're still missing!" Joe concluded.

"That must be the lightning," said Joe. "Whatever that Zapp is, it's got to be powerful stuff."

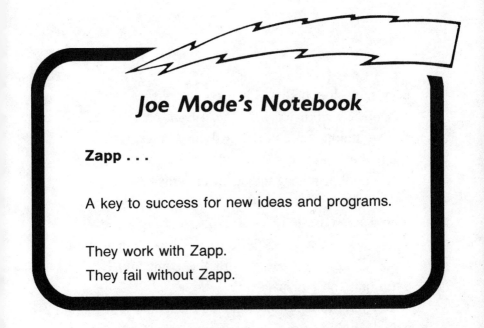

Joe Mode's Notebook

Zapp . . .

A key to success for new ideas and programs.

They work with Zapp.
They fail without Zapp.

But at this point, Joe saw he was still no closer to understanding what Zapp was. He knew he needed help. He decided to violate Ironclad Rule Number One.

9

By now, Ralph Rosco had completed his three-day suspension from work and was back on the job.

The union, of course, had filed a grievance for Ralph, but that was on an endless voyage through the Normal labor-management bureaucracy.

Meanwhile, his output was abysmally low, and he now walked around like a zombie until quitting time. This was not a good period to talk to Ralph about much of anything to do with the company. He had even quit the Normal softball team.

But Joe Mode knew he needed help and that Ralph was the only one in the department who would understand what he was talking about.

So he went to Ralph one day near quitting time.

"Look, Ralph, I want to figure out what that lightning was in Lucy Storm's department. I can't do it on my own, and I was wondering if you'd help me."

"You want *me* to help *you?* Forget it!" cried Ralph.

"OK," said Joe. "I admit you got a bad break. But if you help me out on this, I'll submit your gadget to the management committee."

"Take it to the Normal management committee? Ha!" said Ralph. "Don't make me laugh! They won't do anything, and if they do, they'll give it to some engineers who don't care anything about it."

The man was smarter than Joe Mode had thought.

So Joe said, "But think about it—to help me, you'll of course have to put your Ralpholator back together. You can start using it again and it'll be with my blessing."

"Well . . ." said Ralph.

"And if we can figure out what the lightning is and what makes it go Zapp, we can use it here in our department, and you'll have been a part of that."

"Well . . ." said Ralph.

"And later on I'll even try to get you some company money so *you* can keep developing your machine. What do you say? Are we going to work together on this?"

"Well . . ." said Ralph. "OK!"

Then they shook hands, both genuinely excited. And at that moment, had they been able to observe what was going on in the 12th Dimension, they would have seen a very small bolt of lightning flash between them.

10

The very next day, Ralph reassembled the Ralpholator, fired it up, and vanished into the 12th Dimension.

He started wandering around. Everything and everybody in Dept N was about the same as that first morning—dim and gloomy with all the charm of a minimum security prison.

In the midst of this was Joe Mode, dressed that day (to the eyes of those in the 12th Dimension) in cowboy hat, boots and spurs, and toting six-guns, ready to blast anyone who got in his way.

Ralph was about to mosey on over to Dept Z when he saw something he had not noticed on his first visit.

Ralph watched as Joe walked up to Marty, who was still wrapped in mummy tape, and soon after Joe started talking, there was a flash of—well, it was not lightning.

Instead of a flash of light, there was flash of night.

Kind of like blinking your eyes.

And there was a sound.

It did not go Zapp!

It went "Ssssappi"

To Ralph, it kind of sounded like a balloon deflating. After the Sappi happened, Ralph watched Marty get a couple more turns of mummy tape around him, making the light left inside him a shade dimmer.

Then Ralph noticed Becky trying to say something to Joe and Joe walking away, not paying any attention to her.

Sappi

And Becky became even more zombie-like.

Next, Ralph heard Joe tell Phyllis how to do a job she had often done before without bothering to listen to how she thought it should be done.

Sappi

And a fresh new sandbag appeared on the growing fortifications around her desk.

He saw Joe rush over to someone who was having a problem and immediately pull him off the job and start solving the problem himself.

Sappi

But it wasn't just what Joe was doing. Ralph heard some people telling other people not to work so hard—that it was "bad for all of us."

Sappi

He heard one worker telling some others, "That's not our problem. Let the bosses worry about it."

Sappi

What was going on here, Ralph wondered. These were just routine, everyday, *normal* occurrences—nothing that most people would notice.

But when these things happened, people got dimmer and slower instead of brighter and faster.

Sometimes, a few new stones would appear on the maze of walls crisscrossing the department, or a new chain would wrap itself around someone's arm or leg, or some other constraint would form.

Whatever was happening, it was keeping people divided and confined, draining their energy or damming it up so it couldn't be used.

And Joe Mode was a big part of it. He went through the day Sapping people left and right.

"He's like a black hole, absorbing energy from everyone who works for him," thought Ralph.

These things were not just in Dept N. Ralph wandered through the Normal Company, and saw Sappi happening lots of places and lots of ways.

By the end of the day, throughout most of Normal, the majority of people were dull, de-energized. When the light from the opening doors streaked in at quitting time, everybody bolted for it, glad that the day was over.

Ralph watched them go, rushing for the fix of energy they needed from home and family and the things they did after work. He wandered back through the fog toward Dept N. When he got there, he saw Joe was in trouble.

It was Joe Mode alone in the midst of an enormous cloud of flashing night. He was beaten and bruised, cowboy hat lost, standing his ground as jaws and claws came out of the fog from all directions. He had been bravely firing away with his six-guns at this many-faced thing. Though his bullets had wounded some of the monsters, there were many more than he could shoot at, and his guns were now empty.

What was this thing confronting Joe? Ralph stood and watched him fight his losing battle. And then Ralph had a gut hunch what it was.

It was everything Joe had Sapped from everyone else. What Joe had taken away, had not shared, was now beating him. What was it?

It was Responsibility.

It was Authority.

It was Identity.

It was Energy.

It was Power.

II

Of course, Joe Mode did not believe any of this about Sappi and the cowboy hat and six-guns.

"Then go take a look for yourself," Ralph said. "It's not just in our department, it's in lots of places."

Joe took a look the very next day. Invisible to the normal world, he walked through the company.

He saw a group of industrial engineers making a job so simple that the people doing the job could not understand why it was important—it had no meaning for them.

Sappi

He saw a boss taking all the credit for a good idea— one that his assistant had come up with.

Sappi

Walking down the hall, Joe saw a small patch of night roiling on the wall. It turned out to be a bulletin board with a posted copy of the latest memo from the Normal management committee. "Henceforth," the memo read, "the morning arrival times of all office employees will be recorded by the receptionist and monitored by management."

Sappi

Joe went into marketing and found a salesperson talking to an angry customer. Tiny beads of sweat were breaking out upon the salesperson's forehead, because he had no training in handling difficult customers, no knowledge of how to fix the customer's problem, and no authority to do much of anything except sit there and take it.

Sappi

Coming up the stairwell were two people talking about being passed over for promotion in favor of someone with less experience and job skills.

"Doesn't surprise me," one was saying. "In this company, it doesn't matter how good you are; it's who you play golf with."

And the other nodded. "Yeah, why bother? Office politics—that's what counts."

Sappi Sappii

Joe Mode went out into the Normal manufacturing plant. He saw a manager, a supervisor, a technician, and an operator standing by a disassembled machine.

"I can clear the feeder and get it running, but it'll probably jam up again," said the technician.

"This keeps happening every couple weeks," said the operator.

"We need to take a day and fix it right," said the supervisor.

"No, we don't have time for that," said the manager. "Clear it and get the run started again."

The manager walked away, and the technician said, "Typical. They never give us time to solve the problem."

"What's the use," the operator agreed.

Then the supervisor looked at the back of the manager and muttered to himself, "He doesn't care about quality—or any of my problems for that matter."

Sappi Sappii Sappiii

Joe Mode continued his tour. Overall, he saw lots of Sapping and not very much Zapping going on.

When Joe came back to the normal world, he sat down with Ralph, and together they came up with quite a list of what Sapps people.

Joe Mode's Notebook

Examples of what Sapps people:

- Confusion
- Lack of trust
- Not being listened to
- No time to solve problems
- Bureaucratic office politics
- Someone solving problems for you
- No time to work on bigger issues
- Not knowing whether you are succeeding
- Across-the-board rules and regulations
- A boss taking credit for others' ideas
- Not enough resources to do the job well
- Believing that you can't make a difference
- A job simplified to the point that it has no meaning
- People treated exactly the same, like interchangeable parts

"Look," Joe said after scanning the list. "Don't a lot of these have things in common?"

"Most of these have to do with confidence and trust—or rather the lack of them," said Ralph.

"And esteem and control," said Joe Mode.

"If the lack of those Sapps us," said Ralph, "I wonder what more confidence and trust, and higher esteem and control will do?"

They each looked at the other. Had they found the secret?

It was about then that Joe and Ralph began to realize that Sappi and Zapp! were halves of the same idea.

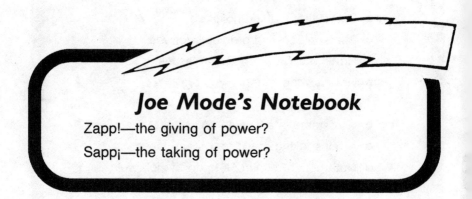

Joe Mode's Notebook

Zapp!—the giving of power?
Sappi—the taking of power?

12

Ralph spent the next morning invisibly observing Dept Z from the 12th Dimension.

There was plenty of Zapp going around. But it was hard to see why it was happening. Still, he observed some big differences between Lucy's Dept Z and Joe's Dept N.

In Dept Z, people pretty much ran their own jobs. They could make lots of decisions on their own.

In Dept N, everybody had to check with Joe before doing anything.

People in Dept Z acted as if their jobs were important to them and they were important to their jobs.

People in Dept N acted as if their jobs didn't much matter in the scheme of things.

Whether things went right or went wrong, people took it a bit personally in Dept Z.

It was hard to know how things were going in Dept N,

and, no matter how things went, people thought it was bad to take it personally.

People in Dept Z were so involved with their work, they talked about it with each other—sometimes even on their breaks.

People in Dept N would look at you funny if you said anything about your work that indicated personal involvement. The only acceptable conversation topics during breaks were softball, vacation plans, and vegetable gardens.

In Lucy Storm's department, the day ended when you finished that day's jobs. Then each person left with a sense of accomplishment, tired but still energized—and *wanting* to come back tomorrow.

In Joe Mode's department, the day ended when the buzzer sounded, and people hurried out counting the days left to the weekend, retirement, or both.

After a while in the 12th Dimension, Ralph began to get an idea of how people felt when they were Sapped and when they were Zapped.

Joe Mode's Notebook

Examples of what Zapps people:

Responsibility
Trust
Being listened to
Teams
Solving problems as a team
Praise
Recognition for ideas
Knowing why you're important to the
   organization
Flexible controls
Direction (clear key result areas,
   measurements, goals)
Knowledge (skills, training,
   information, goals)
Support (approval, coaching,
   feedback, encouragement)
Resources readily available
Upward and downward
   communications

Joe Mode's Notebook

When you have been *Sapped,* you feel like . . .

Your job belongs to the company.

You are just doing whatever you are told.

Your job doesn't really matter.

You don't know how well you're doing.

You always have to keep your mouth shut.

Your job is something different from who you are.

You have little or no control over your work.

When you have been *Zapped,* you feel like . . .

Your job belongs to you.

You are responsible.

Your job counts for something.

You know where you stand.

You have some say in how things are done.

Your job is a part of who you are.

You have some control over your work.

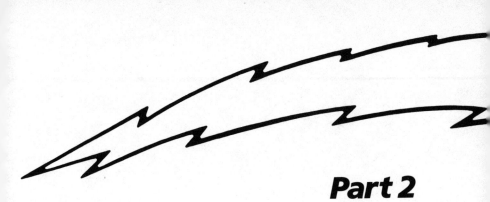

Part 2

The Zapping
of Dept N

13

Joe Mode's phone began to ring.

"Hi, it's me," said Ralph when Joe answered.

"It's about time you got back," said Joe.

"But I'm not back yet. I'm standing next to you in your office in the 12th Dimension, only you can't see me."

"Then how are you talking to me?"

"With my new cellular Ral-phone, the only telephone that works in the 12th Dimension," said Ralph. "I invented the new back-pack model so I wouldn't have to keep coming back to the normal world to talk to you."

"OK, great. Now what else have you found out?" asked Joe, who, as usual, had no time for chitchat.

So Ralph gave him a full report on how Sapped people feel and how Zapped people feel.

"That's it!" said Joe Mode after Ralph explained what he had seen.

"What's it?" asked Ralph.

"What you just said. It's simple. Zapped people own their jobs, they're responsible, they make decisions on their own—right? So I'll have everybody here be like that."

"But how?" asked Ralph.

"Well, of course, I'll just call a meeting and tell them that's the way it's going to be," said Joe Mode.

And pushing all doubts aside, Joe went around the department and told everyone to drop what they were doing and come to an important five-minute meeting.

"OK, listen up everybody," said Joe when they were assembled. "From now on, you own your jobs. They're all yours. I'm not making any decisions for you. You're responsible for everything that has to do with your job. You can each decide how you want to get your work done. You're in control. From this moment forward, I have complete confidence in all of you. Oh, by the way, your jobs are important, so start acting like it. Any questions?"

Of course there were none because nobody understood what in the world he was talking about.

"Good. Everybody back to work," said Joe.

Having made his speech, Joe Mode went back to his office, put his feet up on his desk, and daydreamed fantasies of management congratulations and pay raises.

Half an hour later, Ralph called and said, "Joe, I hate to tell you this, but things are not going very well."

"What? Isn't everybody Zapped after my speech?" asked Joe.

"You'd better take a look for yourself."

Indeed, when Joe stepped out of his office, he saw that Dept N was in a state of chaos.

Given the power to make their own decisions, some people had decided to take a break for the rest of the day.

All around the department, arguments had broken out among those who were working. Each person wanted to do things *his* way or *her* way.

But most people were carrying on exactly as before, as if Joe's proclamation had never been made.

After spending all their working lives in a state of Sapp, nobody knew what to do.

Joe called another important five-minute meeting and said, "Remember what I said earlier? Well, forget it. From now on, I'm back in charge."

Now everyone was doubly Sapped.

The whole matter was trickier than Joe Mode had figured. He retreated to his office and made an entry in his notebook.

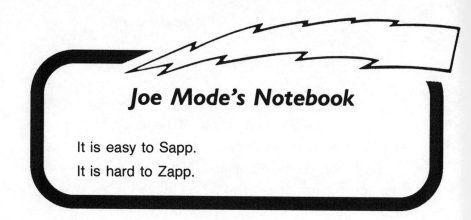

Joe Mode's Notebook

It is easy to Sapp.
It is hard to Zapp.

"Now what do I do?!" he wondered aloud as he paced back and forth. "If I can't *talk* people into being Zapped, how can I make it happen?"

A moment later the phone rang. It was Ralph, who was still in the 12th Dimension and able to hear everything Joe was saying and see everything he had going on in his head.

"You know, Joe, I've never seen Lucy try to *talk* people into being Zapped. I don't think that's how she does it."

"Then what does she do?" Joe asked.

"Well . . ." said Ralph. "I'm not sure exactly."

"OK, we're going to figure this out one way or another," said Joe. "You go down the hall and find Lucy and follow her around. Find out *exactly* what she does."

And Ralph did just that.

An hour later, Joe's phone rang again; it was Ralph with his first observation to report.

Ralph had been watching Lucy and he noticed that whenever she talked to someone, she didn't put the person down or make the person feel inferior. Even if there was a problem, she said what she had to say so that people still felt if not great, at least OK about themselves. That is, she always maintained or enhanced a person's *self-esteem.*

"OK, I'll try that out," said Joe. "You follow me now and watch what happens."

Joe thought for a moment and then went out into the department. The first person he came to was Marty.

"You know, Marty, you're a very snappy dresser," said Joe. "I especially like how your socks always match and how your shirt and pants never clash."

Then Joe saw Dan and said, "Dan, you play a fantastic game of softball."

To this, Dan said, "Gee, thanks, Joe. Do you really think so?"

"Sure I do. But, you know, Dan, you screwed up royally on that job you did yesterday. I suggest you shape up and never let it happen again. I'd hate for the department to lose its best softball player."

Then Joe went back to his office and waited for Ralph to call and tell him how he did.

"When you talked to Marty, nothing happened. No lightning, no Zapp, nothing," said Ralph. "And when you talked to Dan, you actually Sapped him."

"Why? I said nice things to both of them. Didn't that do anything for their self-esteem?"

"But, Joe, you didn't say anything positive about their *work*. Lucy doesn't go out of her way just to tell people they look nice or that she likes the way they play softball. She talks about things they're doing on the job. And, remember, she never puts people down, even if there is a problem."

"OK," said Joe. "Let me try it one more time."

He went back out again, found Marty, and said, "Marty, I like how you keep your work area clean. You're very well organized, and I'm sure that helps you do quality work and get it done faster. Keep it up."

Then he found Dan and said, "Dan, what I was really trying to say earlier was that I think you're usually a first-rate worker. What happened yesterday was a serious mistake, but I hope you'll keep delivering the kind of work you generally turn out."

At this, Dan nodded and said, "I'll try not to let it happen again."

"OK," said Joe. "You're a good man and that's all I can ask."

After each of these, Ralph saw little flickers of lightning. They were small, barely visible, but they were there. He called Joe.

"Bingo!" said Ralph. "You did it! You Zapped 'em!"

A few days passed, and Joe kept using words that would maintain people's self-esteem when he talked to them about their work.

In fact, he even went out of his way to build self-esteem, making a point to try to say something constructive to each person in the department several times every day. After all those years of being Sapped, he reasoned, it was going to take lots of little Zapps to build up a positive charge in people.

But the quality of what he said to them was also important. People could tell when something Joe said was not sincere or was undeserved. In those cases, the Zapp quickly turned into a Sapp!

As time went by, Ralph saw the little flickers of lightning in Dept N grow brighter. Still, they were small, nothing like the brilliance or size of the Zapps in Dept Z.

"You did a good job observing what Lucy was doing," Joe said to Ralph. "I know we're on the right track. But maintaining self-esteem must be only the first step. Why don't you keep looking and see what else she does."

Joe Mode's Notebook

1st step
of Zapp:

Maintain
Self-esteem

14

The next day, Ralph was over in Dept Z and all the amazing things were going on as usual. Monsters were being tamed, battles won, new vistas opened, new visions created. And the incredible lightning energizing all of this was Zapping brilliantly from Lucy to her people.

Then Ralph noticed something he thought was rather odd. While some of the lightning flashed when Lucy talked, often she would just be there with someone, seemingly doing nothing—and Zapp!—a little bolt of lightning would jump from her to the next person. It was as if Lucy could generate a Zapp just by standing next to someone.

By now, though, Ralph knew that Zapp did not happen by itself. Lucy had to be doing something. He watched her some more.

Then he noticed Lucy was letting the other person

do the talking. She would be standing or sitting nearby, often a hand on her chin, eyes focused on the other person, sometimes her head angled to one side. And as she did this, a little Zapp would pass between her and the person talking.

What was she doing, Ralph wondered.

Why, of course! She was *listening!*

He got on the Ral-phone, dialed Joe Mode, and told him: Listening to people is another way to Zapp them.

"So what's the big deal about that?" asked Joe Mode. "I listen to people—all the time."

Ralph did not say anything.

"Don't I listen to people?" asked Joe.

Still Ralph said nothing.

"WELL, DON'T I?"

"Lots of times I'm not sure, Joe," said Ralph.

"And why not?"

"Because you're doing other things while I'm talking, or you don't let me finish what I have to say, or you'll change the subject when I do finish," said Ralph.

Joe took this in. Then he said, "OK, but how do you know *she's* really listening?"

"Well, because she's looking at the person, and she's nodding her head like she understands."

"Oh, hell's bells, Ralph! My kids do that! And I never know if they're listening or not," said Joe.

"Wait a minute, I know," said Ralph, remembering something else Lucy did each time she listened, something which made the lightning glow brighter. "When the other person was done talking, she repeated a little summary of what had been said."

"So she is listening," thought Joe.

"All right, let me try it," he said to Ralph.

And he did.

As soon as he stepped out of his office, Phyllis came over to him and started to talk about a problem she was having.

Joe stood in front of her.

He looked her in the eye.

He focused his full attention on her.

He nodded his head as she made a point.

But after a few seconds, he found it was hard to listen well. Even though Phyllis got to the point quickly, Joe's own thoughts kept coming faster than her words. His own thoughts seemed to cover up what he was hearing. If he didn't push his own thoughts aside and concentrate on her words, he soon did not hear what she was saying.

When Phyllis was finished, Joe tried to summarize what she had said to let her know he had listened. But he found he had only caught the first part of what she had said.

Still, he tried it some more. That was another thing to Joe Mode's credit: he would always keep trying.

As he went through Dept N, he practiced listening to people the rest of the day. And the next day. And the day after that.

After a while, Joe Mode became pretty good at

listening to people. Instead of letting his own thoughts clutter up the message he was hearing, he kept his mind busy with keeping a mental list of each point the person made. Then it was easy to give back a short summary. If he got a point wrong, the person to whom he had been listening could make the point clear.

Aside from letting people know he was paying attention to what they said, he also began to understand what was really going on in Dept N. Meanwhile, Ralph each day would turn on the Ralpholator after he had finished his work and go see how Joe was coming along.

As you might imagine, Ralph was getting a big kick out of checking up on his boss. At first, Ralph, who had his cynical side, figured that Joe Mode would *never* really listen to anybody. He even thought he might have the grim pleasure at the end of the week of telling Joe Mode that the Zapps were not happening, that Joe would never learn.

Ralph was wrong.

In fact, to his surprise, Joe was doing quite well. Just by maintaining self-esteem and by listening to people, the Sapps had become far fewer and the Zapps far more common. There was a weak but definite glow now around Dept N.

Ralph did not even have to be in the 12th Dimension to notice it. There was less tension in Dept N.

Problems seemed to get sorted out a little faster. The work flow seemed to be a little smoother.

And yet, he did have to report that the Zapps Joe Mode gave by listening were not of the magnitude Lucy Storm gave. When Joe Mode listened, the Zapp would start to grow and glow as hers did. But, then, Joe Mode would walk away, and the Zapp would vanish. Sometimes it even became a Sapp!

One day Ralph was having some trouble with "the guts" of a normalator. So Ralph told Joe about it.

"I've worked all morning on this, but I just don't have the tools to fix the problem," said Ralph, sounding extremely frustrated.

Joe Mode listened dutifully, nodded his head, and even repeated an accurate summary of what Ralph had said.

Then Joe Mode pivoted and walked away.

"Hey, Joe, wait a minute," Ralph said.

Joe walked back and said, "What?"

"Is that it?" asked Ralph. "Is that all you're going to do?"

"What else do you expect?" asked Joe.

"At least some kind of response," said Ralph.

Joe was puzzled. Hadn't he done the enZapping thing? Hadn't he listened?

And Ralph suddenly understood why Joe was not generating the maximum charge when he listened.

"Joe, I think there are two parts to this," said

Ralph. "One part is listening. The other part is responding. You've got the listening part fine, but you often don't respond."

And Joe said, "OK, how about if I say, 'I heard you. Now get back to work.' "

"That makes me feel like you just want to get rid of me," said Ralph. "It's a Sappi"

"But I wasn't just trying to get rid of you," said Joe. "In fact, I was going to try to get you some help."

"Then why don't you tell me that," said Ralph.

To which Joe said, "All right, then, how about if I say, 'I heard what you said. I'll get you the help you need.' "

Ralph considered this. "Well, that's a little better, but somehow it feels as though there is still something missing. I mean, I've spent the whole morning trying to work this out, and you didn't even acknowledge that."

Then Joe Mode suddenly got it. He had listened and responded to the words Ralph had said, but not to the *tone* in which Ralph had said them.

"OK, *I sense that you're very frustrated,*" said Joe Mode. "Why don't you work on something else, and I'll get you the help you need."

And when he said that, there was a Zapp, one that lasted longer and glowed brighter than what had been before. Joe knew from that point on that he not only had to listen, he had to *respond with empathy.*

From then on, after Joe listened, he tried to give the

person an appropriate response, and to respond to more than just the actual, factual words, but to all the things behind the words.

This meant Joe Mode had to pay attention to the total context of what was being said, and to take into account not only the person's tone of voice, but things like body language, facial expressions, and events leading up to the discussion.

For instance, when someone would come to Joe with a problem, Joe would often say something like, "OK, I understand you're upset. Let's try to work something out."

When someone would come to Joe with a request, he might say something like, "I sense that this is important to you. We'll see what we can do."

Of course there were lots of times when nothing could be done. Problems sometimes had to be endured rather than solved; requests sometimes had to be denied.

In those cases, Joe would say something like, "I know this is tough for you, but there's nothing we can do right now. Meanwhile, it's important to the whole department that you hang in there and do the best you can."

Even this registered a Zapp. Because the people then knew that at least they had been heard and considered. And they knew their boss was with them and not against them.

Joe Mode's Notebook

**2nd step
of Zapp:**

Listen and
Respond
with Empathy

15

Some say it came from Engineering, that it was the creation of Bob, a junior-grade designer whose mind was numbed by the spell of an evil wizard from another galaxy.

Some say it came from the Executive Suite, where it had been sleeping for several years under a vice president's desk—hibernating until awakened by the fanfare accompanying a management proclamation of new corporate policy.

And some say it had been in Operations all along, small and cute at first, but growing, slinking about by night, gorging itself on memos, reports, and other combustibles.

Wherever it came from, it was a big mother dragon. And it stalked the Normal halls in the 12th Dimension looking for places to lay eggs.

Ralph saw it one day. He was taking a reading with

his newly developed Zappometer (pronounced "Zapp-aw'-met-er"), which measures Sappi-Zapp! ratios and lightning levels.

Dept N had become a much brighter place. In the past week, Ralph had observed a 1:2 ratio in Sappi-Zapp! frequency as well as an improvement of 14 bolts in the department's average Zapp charge.

Ralph watched Joe Mode walking through Dept N. Joe still had his cowboy hat and spurs, but he seldom reached for his six-guns anymore. As he said and did enZapping things—maintaining each person's self-esteem, listening to each person, and responding with empathy—little forks of lightning flashed between him and the others.

Things had improved, but the lightning still did not reach very far or last very long. When Joe was not around, people quickly got dull. Their glow would fade, like red-hot steel cooling down and turning gray. Unlike in Dept Z, the Zapp did not interconnect them and the charge of energy never reached the threshold to become self-sustaining.

As Ralph was considering this, he felt a tremor in the floor. And a moment later another tremor. And another. Then from around the corner came the purple, scaly snout of the dragon.

Like all industrial dragons, this one was invisible to the normal world, but its effects were quite real.

A swipe of its talons, and data in the Normal computer would be randomly trashed.

One switch of its tail, and a critical machine would break down.

Wherever this dragon breathed, fires broke out—a thousand parts would arrive late and a third of them would be defective.

The dragon squeezed its wings through the main door of Dept N, took a deep breath, and—whoosh—a long stream of red and orange arched across the department, igniting one of the normalators, which burst into a tower of flames.

Joe Mode, who had been in the middle of responding with empathy to something Dan had said, immediately broke off in mid-sentence and rushed to the fire, his cowboy hat bending and twisting as he hurried until it became a white fireman's helmet.

Marty, who was closest to the conflagration, had already grabbed a 12th Dimension fire hose and was about to turn on the water, but Joe Mode got there and wrestled it away from him.

Sappi—and Marty's Zapp charge, such as it was, got grounded out.

"Stand aside!" said Mode. "Everybody out of the way!"

Joe stood there figuring out how to turn on the hose while the flames rose higher.

Meanwhile, the dragon wandered down the aisle, flicked its long forked tongue, and the data disk in Mrs. Estello's word processor went up in smoke.

Of course, Mrs. Estello had no idea what to do. Her

job was just to type, wasn't it? So she got up and took the smoking disk down the aisle to Joe Mode, who, of course, was too busy wielding the fire hose to listen to her.

Sappi

So Mrs. Estello left the smoking data disk in Joe's office and went out for a break.

And the dragon roared again. More red and orange streaked through the air, and another fire erupted on the far side of the department. Then the dragon whipped its tail around to spread the flames.

Now three or four little fires were beginning to burn, and Joe was too busy fighting the first fire to notice them. Actually, he was too busy enjoying the fight. It was fun being a fireman. In fact, he was not about to hand his hose or fireman's helmet over to anybody. Why should he? Wasn't this his job?

He just about had the first fire doused when he saw the smoke from the others. All of a sudden, fire fighting wasn't so much fun. He tried rushing back and forth between them, spraying one, then the next. But as soon as he turned his back, the fires burned up and up and out of control.

Ralph watched, waiting for someone to help Joe, but no one did. Joe Mode may have been giving them little Zapps now and then, but who were they to face invisible dragons and raging fires? Against those, they were still just a bunch of Sapped zombies.

All but oblivious to Joe's heroics, they kept doing what they normally did, or just stood around and basked in the heat while Joe ran from fire to fire and Mrs. Estello, back from her break, tagged along with her charred data disk waiting for him to tell her what to do.

And the dragon grinned.

Ralph put in a call on the Ral-phone, but Joe, of course, was too busy to take it. When Ralph came back to the normal world, they finally got together in Ralph's work area. Joe came in as sweaty and tired as a fireman could be—and more than a little impatient and frustrated.

"Ralph, this Zapp stuff isn't working," he complained. "I've got five normalators out there that won't pass inspection. Paperwork is backed up because Mrs. Estello doesn't have enough Zapp to figure out what's wrong with her word processor disk. And I'm too busy solving all the problems around here to Zapp anyone!"

But Ralph, after some talking, persuaded Joe to come have a look at what the dragon was doing.

By then, having had its fun, the dragon had deposited a few eggs to hatch sometime later, incubated by the heat of smoldering fires, and had wandered on.

Its trail was easy to follow. In department after department, the supervisors and managers were the ones fighting the fires, figuring out the problems, straightening out the dragon's mayhem.

In one department, a smart manager, in addition to wielding his own hose, had organized a bucket brigade, and was directing the zombie workers in what to do. But the Sapped zombies did not have much interest in the buckets, nor in whether the fires were put out or not.

When the manager was called away to hose down yet another fire, he neglected to tell the bucket brigade to put the water *on the fire.* And since zombies can't think for themselves or make decisions on their own, they splashed the water every which way. They were tripping over the buckets, spilling water on one another, bumping into each other. All of which was hysterical to the dragon.

Then, from down the corridor, came the sirens. It was the executive fire truck, gleefully driven by Mary Ellen Krabofski herself, trollish as ever, her fire engine-red fingernails curled around the steering wheel.

Riding the truck with her was the entire executive volunteer fire brigade. "Fire Expert," it said in bold gold letters on each of their slickers.

Mary Ellen brought the fire truck screeching to a halt and hopped out. The first thing she did was run over and take the fire hose out of the department manager's hands.

"Gimme that," she said.

Sappi

And what did the expert fire fighters do? First, they ran around the truck half a dozen times chasing everybody away.

Sappi Sappi Sappi

Then *they* grabbed the buckets and started splashing water.

From down the hall where the fire truck had come, there now came a clatter of hooves. Yes, it was a knight in shining armor on a white horse.

The knight rode up to Mary Ellen.

"Hi, I'm Hugh Galahad, Mother Dragon Specialist," he said.

"About time you got here," she said.

"Wow, looks like you've got a big one," said the knight.

"We *know* that," said Mary Ellen gesturing with the fire hose in hand. "Now go slay it or I'll rust your armor."

Without even pausing to ask anyone where the dragon might be, the knight dropped his visor, lowered the point of his lance, and charged into the smoke. Unfortunately, his visibility limited by the tiny slits in the visor, the knight galloped right past the dragon and speared two of the workers.

And the dragon slipped out the fire escape. It headed for the executive floor, figuring to spit some sparks under the carpets while no one was around.

Ralph and Joe followed at a discreet distance.

Of course, Dept Z was not exempt from visitations by the monsters and calamities of business. Eventually the mother dragon came down the hall toward Dept Z, as invisible to Lucy Storm as it was to anyone in the normal world.

Joe and Ralph arrived just after the dragon had entered Dept Z. As elsewhere, it huffed and puffed and breathed fire right into the middle of things.

But Lucy did not try to solve the problem of the dragon on her own. She did not put on armor and fight the dragon, or put on a fire helmet and fight the fire.

At the first whiff of smoke, she went to the person nearest the fire hose and, lightning bolt forming in her hand, said, "We have a problem. I'd like your help. . . ."

Zapp!

And *that* person picked up the fire hose and figured out how to fight the fire—while Lucy pulled some others together into a group and said, "We have a big problem and I'd like all of your help. . . ."

Zapp! Zapp! Zapp!

Those people then started talking among themselves about what to do, while Lucy went back to check on the fire. By the time she returned, they had an action plan worked out.

At a nod from Lucy, some of them put on fire helmets. Then Lucy got them some fire extinguishers and they went to work on the new fires the dragon was starting.

The rest of the group put on armor and went to chase the dragon. Unlike many previous dragons, this one was too big for them to slay or tame on their own, but they did succeed in harassing it into leaving.

(And it did not take so very long, because dragons, as you know, prefer dark and foggy places to lay their eggs, and there was too much energy and light in Dept Z for it to linger long or lay many eggs.)

Meanwhile, Lucy had gone around to every other person individually in Dept Z and said, "We're trying to solve a problem and I'd like your help. . . ."

Zapp!

And each of the people had filled in here and there for the others so that the regular work got done.

After it was gone, it was clear that the dragon had not Sapped the department. With an abundance of Zapp, it had been a lot like fighting fire with fire. In fact, the Zapp now glowed even brighter than before; people were charged up by having met the challenge.

Watching it all, Joe realized that Zapp *did* work. He

simply did not yet have enough of it in his department and he was not yet using it fully.

Just as he and Ralph were about to leave, Hugh Galahad charged into the department. Lucy Storm had to hurry over and grab the reins before he carelessly speared one of *her* workers.

"Whoa!" she said. "Can I help you with something?"

"Don't bother me. I'm on the trail of a big mother dragon," said the knight.

"It was here, but we chased it away," Lucy said.

"What?!" said the knight. "You dealt with it on your own? Impossible!"

"But we did," she said.

And the knight, feeling threatened, said, "Well, you can't do that. You're not allowed! Wait until Ms. Krabofski hears about this!"

Sappi

The knight rode away. But his Sapp was soon overpowered by the Zapp in Dept Z. No single Sapp of a mere threatened knight could take away the energy of what they had achieved.

Joe and Ralph went back to Dept N, where Joe called Marty, Mrs. Estello, and the others together.

He began by saying, "I'd like your help in solving a problem. . . ."

Zapp!

Joe Mode's Notebook

3rd step
of Zapp:

Ask for Help
in Solving
Problems

(Seek ideas, suggestions,
and information)

16

So why are we having so many fires—excuse me, *problems* around here?" Joe Mode asked everyone in the meeting where he first asked for help.

At first, everyone was too Sapped to talk. After a minute of silence, Joe nearly threw up his hands and dismissed the meeting.

But, instead, on a hunch, he tossed out a first-level Zapp to the group. He told them he thought they were all reasonable and smart people, that every day they saw what was going on, and that they probably had some good notions about what the problem was.

Marty was the first to venture a guess—which Becky promptly disagreed with and put forth a theory of her own. Then Luis had an idea, and before long, lots of people were talking.

Joe then Zapped them some more by listening to what each of them had to say and making a list of their theories of what might be happening.

Finally, they narrowed the list, went out and tested

those ideas and, sure enough, one of them turned out to be the cause of the problem.

"See, we've got too much fliptorque in the rama-dram," said Dirk, who had first suggested that possibility.

"That must be it," said Joe Mode. "OK. Thanks for your input. Everybody back to work."

And everybody nodded and walked away. But as they turned their backs, what happened in the 12th Dimension?

Sappi

Well, Joe Mode came up with a solution (a brilliant one, he thought) to the fliptorque problem. But when he went out and told everybody what it was and what they had to do, they looked at him with zombie eyes.

Indeed, Joe Mode's solution did pretty much solve the fliptorque problem—when people remembered to do what Joe had told them to do. But his idea did not make life easier for anybody, and nobody was very interested in whether it worked or not. Soon new fires spread in the ramadrams.

Joe talked to Ralph, for by now Joe had come to trust Ralph and his opinions.

"Ralph, how come my brilliant solution isn't working?" he asked.

Ralph had a fairly good idea what was wrong. Indeed, Joe had Zapped everyone by asking them to help him find the problem. Then Joe Mode unintentionally had Sapped them when he took the problem away from them and solved it himself.

"But they can't come up with solutions," argued Joe Mode. "It'll be a waste of time. They don't have my experience, my technical know-how, my grasp of the big picture."

"Oh?" said Ralph.

"Anyway, coming up with solutions is *my* job, isn't it?"

"Joe, the plain fact is that you've still got fires out there," said Ralph. "Your idea may have been brilliant, but nobody else had a stake in making it work. They didn't own it, you did. It wasn't *their* solution."

Grumbling to himself, Joe finally admitted that Ralph might be right. He told Ralph to go have a look in the 12th Dimension while he talked to the people again. At the meeting this time he asked for help not just in finding the problem, but in coming up with a solution.

It was Luis, one of the younger employees in Dept N, who came up with the best idea. He said, "Why don't we just keep the whamnuts loose and that'll keep the fliptorque down in the ramadrams."

Everyone, even a very surprised Joe Mode, knew immediately that this was a great idea. The group talked about the best ways to keep the whamnuts loose, and there were Zapps all around.

"OK, thanks a lot for that great idea. I appreciate

your help," Joe said, and then with a wave good-bye added, *"I'll take it from here."*

As soon as he said that, Ralph, who was watching this from the 12th Dimension, saw the lightning, which was glowing brightly among the people in the group, move from them to Joe. Joe Mode once again had taken their lightning—stolen it almost.

Everyone went back to their normal work, and Joe tried to use their idea. In fact, there was no way for Joe Mode to "take it from here" all on his own. *He* was not doing the loosening or tightening of the whamnuts. Other people were.

Joe soon saw that those other people were not very enthusiastic. They just weren't all that interested in whether the whamnuts were loose or tight. Or they didn't understand. Or they privately came up with reasons why this solution wouldn't work. Even though Joe had Zapped them in getting the idea, he Sapped them by disinvolving them in implementing it.

Now the dragon was heard stomping down the hall once more. It came into Dept N and breathed fire all over the place. As usual, everyone stood around waiting for Joe Mode to come and fight the fires. Which he did.

At the end of the day, having enjoyed itself immensely, the dragon wandered on.

Ralph came to Joe and said, "You know, Joe, something isn't right."

"You're telling me!" said Joe.

"Don't you remember the very first time we saw Lucy Storm? Remember who fought the dragon?"

"It was that guy who worked for her," said Joe.

"That's right," said Ralph. "And do you remember what happened when the new dragon showed up?"

"She got together a team to fight the dragon," said Joe Mode.

"And do you remember who *did not* fight the dragon?"

"Well, sure," said Joe Mode. "It was Lucy Storm who did not fight the dragon."

As soon as he said that, he understood. Lucy Storm had offered help, but had not taken away from the individual or the group the challenge of fighting the dragon and its fires. She had left the responsibility with them.

The next day, Joe Mode called a third meeting. This time he went over the problem again and the group discussed the solution. But after they had discussed the solution, Joe Mode said, "Let's talk about what *you* need to make this work."

This time the Zapp stayed with the people in the group. They owned the problem, the idea for solving it, *and* the challenge of making the idea succeed.

In fact, this was a little too much Zapp for a few of the people. After years of Sapp, suddenly having a bolt of lightning thrown at them was very frightening. Their immediate reaction was to try to get rid of it—to brush it off or throw the lightning back to Joe and the others in the group.

Joe had to react quickly to make sure they would not Sapp themselves. He listened to their fears and then said some things to maintain their self-esteem and build their confidence. He also instinctively lowered the voltage for these people, giving them smaller bolts of Zapp, which would not blow their fuses.

But most of the people were happy to accept the Zapp given them. They carried it away with them back to their workplaces, and it flashed and flickered among them even as they did their normal work.

By the time the dragon next made its rounds, everybody knew what to do as soon as its ugly head came around the corner. Rather than waiting for Joe to do something, they picked up the new fire hoses, armor, and swords they had requested and which Joe had procured for them—and went after the dragon themselves.

Things were not perfect, mind you. Dan kept tripping over his hose. Marty busily dealt with a tiny fire while behind him a huge one raged out of control. The dragon chasers were very clumsy with their weapons. And through the crisis, poor old Mrs. Estello kept typing away and wondering what all the excitement was about.

But this day it was the people in Dept N who had the good time rather than the dragon. And the dragon soon left. The fires were put out very quickly.

"We did it!" they all said to each other.

Watching what happened from the 12th Dimension, Ralph saw the department light up like dawn. And that was how Joe Mode learned to generate the electric soul of Zapp in the normal people of Dept N.

Joe Mode's Notebook

The Soul of Zapp!

Offer Help
Without Taking
Responsibility

Joe Mode's Notebook

The first three steps
to Zapping others . . .

1. Maintain Self-esteem.

2. Listen and Respond
   with Empathy.

3. Ask for Help in Solving
   Problems.

. . . lead to the Soul of Zapp:

Offer Help
Without Taking
Responsibility

17

So it came to pass that Dept N began to experience the power of Zapp. People began to feel the lightning in their work. Together, they had turned away a big mama dragon and battled its raging fires. They felt energized about their work—some of them for the first time ever.

And how did Joe Mode feel? Did he feel like a hero? Did he feel terrific?

No, he began to feel more and more nervous, scared, and confused.

It was as if everything he had learned over the past few weeks was fine for dealing with a crisis, but now that the dragon was leaving them alone, he wanted to stop and forget about it.

Ralph noticed the change.

"Joe, what's wrong?" he asked. "You look worried. You're not Zapping people the way you could be. What's holding you back?"

Joe muttered some feeble excuses, but Ralph kept pressing him until he said what was really bothering him.

"To Zapp people in a big way, I have to encourage them to get involved and take responsibility, right?" said Joe.

"Right."

"If I let other people take the responsibility, how do I know they'll live up to it?"

"Beats me. I guess you have to trust them," said Ralph.

"Trust them? That's easy for you to say. Remember when I tried letting everybody make their own decisions? It was a disaster!" said Joe Mode.

"That's true," Ralph agreed.

"So how can I control what's going on?" asked Joe. "What if nothing gets done on time? What if things get done but they're the wrong things? What if somebody does something I don't know about and everything gets screwed up? Who is Mary Ellen Krabofski going to yell at?"

"You," admitted Ralph.

"Right. Me. I'll get yelled at. I'll get the blame. And, if the screw-up is bad enough, I'll get fired," said Joe Mode. "Sure I'd like people to be Zapped—but not if it's going to get me in trouble."

"Look, you Zapped me when you asked for help figuring out how Lucy ran Dept Z. You gave me responsibility. Did I let you down?" Ralph argued.

"No, but I knew what you were doing," said Joe. "Well?"

Had you been in the 12th Dimension, you would have seen a new sun rise inside Joe Mode's head. Of course! Offering help to people in the department in part meant staying in touch with them, *knowing* what they were doing, what they planned to do, keeping them on track.

In short, there still had to be control. But how could he use control so as not to Sapp everyone?

Within five minutes, Joe got everything he needed to figure it out.

First, the phone rang. It was the Shipping Dept. saying they were having trouble with "the guts" of one of the normalators they were about to send out. Could Joe do something to get it fixed before three o'clock?

Then Phyllis came in and reminded Joe that Mary Ellen Krabofski needed next year's budget figures by the end of the day.

Next, Becky came by and asked how many dooverdogs went into a dynadigi.

Then a mail clerk delivered the new tech specs for Normalator Model 303-B, which would have to be routed to everyone in Dept N.

How would Joe handle all these things?

In the old days, Joe Mode would have tried to handle all or most of them himself, and he would have Sapped everyone as he did.

This time, Joe decided to delegate responsibility where it was appropriate.

First, he *referred* Becky to Gary Girder in the Engineering Dept. He knew Gary would know how many dooverdogs in a dynadigi and he could tell her in a second.

Next he went to Ralph and asked for help with the problem in Shipping. He knew he could trust Ralph, so he *delegated the authority* to Ralph to go to Shipping and fix whatever was wrong.

But because it was super critical that the normalator be shipped by three o'clock, Joe set up a *check* with Ralph by asking him to call at two o'clock and give a status report. That way Joe could offer help if Ralph was having difficulty.

(Now, in fact, this kind of control was not a Sapp on Ralph. That's because Ralph, too, understood the importance of the situation. It was actually a Zapp for him to be able to communicate with Joe in case the situation was more than he could handle or to report his success.)

Then Joe had to deal with the distribution of the new tech specs. He asked Marty to handle that. But because Joe knew he could not fully trust Marty's judgment in all matters, he only *delegated the task* of passing out the specs, and said, "Tell everyone that if they have any questions they should come and see me."

In this case, the task was hardly tricky, so there was no need for Marty to check back with Joe.

Finally, there was the budget. Joe recognized that no one else could do the budget. He would have to do it himself. That task he *kept.*

This was how Joe Mode began to understand that control was not absolute. It was not on or off; control was a matter of degree.

And the amount given to others or kept to oneself depended upon the *situation.* Control largely was a question of what to delegate and how often to check on how people were doing.

Joe Mode's Notebook

My choices in delegating responsibility:

- Refer the task to the proper person.

- Delegate authority to carry out the task and make decisions.

- Delegate the task without giving decision-making authority.

- Keep the task.

With delegation comes the need to set up controls.

- A boss who *over*controls Sapps his people.

- A boss who *abandons* control Sapps his people.

- A boss who uses *situational* control Zapps his people.

People only respond negatively to controls when they are inappropriate for the situation.

Joe Mode's Notebook

Sharing responsibility with people does not mean *abandoning* responsibility.

Through Zapp, people gain responsibility in their individual jobs, but I still have the responsibility to . . .

- Know what is going on.
- Set the direction for the department.
- Make the decisions they can't.
- Ensure that people are on course.
- Offer a guiding hand; open doors to clear the way.
- Assess performance.
- Be a smart manager.

18

Joe Mode was seeing lots more initiative and interest on the part of people in Dept N. Trouble was, these revved-up people were charging off on all kinds of different tangents, some of which were not very productive.

The crisis of the ramadram problems had been exciting for people. It had felt, well, kind of like fighting a pitched battle against an invisible dragon and winning. Lots of people secretly hoped something like that would happen again, and Joe found some were still working on the same problem long after it had been solved—while their boring, normal work was being neglected.

Joe Mode's Notebook

- Zapp does not guide action; it excites action.

- To get the job done, I have to channel the action in the right direction.
  But how?

He tried having more meetings so they could talk about what else had to be done in the department, but that in itself became a problem rather than the solution. Meetings took lots of time away from the job, and every time he held one it seemed like Mary Ellen Krabofski would just happen by and wonder why no one was "working." Joe tried to tell her that the meeting was part of the work, but she didn't buy it.

"That's not what we're paying them for," she whined.

Joe was stumped. How could he get the department—as a group and as individuals—to do the right things without having a meeting every ten minutes and without standing behind each of them telling them what to do?

For a while, Joe let people follow whatever initiatives they wanted to take. He thought it would increase their Zapp. So when Luis came to him and said that he and some co-workers wanted to paint the floor around their work area, Joe said OK and helped them get the paint and brushes they needed.

Then Luis came to him and said they wanted to paint the ceiling and would need some drop cloths.

"Why do you want to paint the ceiling?" asked Joe.

"It'll reflect the light better and we'll be more productive," said Luis.

Joe did not think that was a very good reason, but he did not want to Sapp their initiative, so he said OK and helped them get the drop cloths.

Then Luis came back and said they needed more of everything because they wanted to paint the hallway. Again, Joe said OK. But as he was writing up the requisition slip, Phyllis came in and told Joe that half the department had no work to do.

"That's strange," Joe thought. He went out into the department and found a week's worth of work piled high in front of the drop cloths and paint cans in Luis' work area—which was beautiful by now because Luis and the others had done a terrific job.

"Hey, Luis, how come you've got all this work backed up?" asked Joe.

"Because we've been too busy painting so we could be more productive," said Luis.

"But painting isn't what is really important," said Joe.

"It isn't?" asked Luis.

"No, in fact, I'd say it's pretty low on the list of things you could be doing," said Joe.

Luis shook his head, dropped his brush in the paint can, and said, "Well, then, why didn't you tell us what *was* important so we wouldn't waste so much time?"

"Good question," Joe thought.

Sapp!

To make matters even worse, Ralph came in at the end of the day and reported that the Zapp level was down ten bolts and dropping quickly. It seemed that without a dragon to focus their efforts, people were changing things that didn't need to be changed, solving problems that didn't need to be solved, throwing their energy in a thousand different directions and Sapping themselves.

Joe thought for a while. There were many things about Dept N that could be improved, but Joe had no clear objectives. He went to Mary Ellen Krabofski to ask if she could explain what management truly expected from him and Dept N.

But all Mary Ellen said was, "If you don't know your own job, I'm not going to tell you."

Joe retreated to his office. If management was not

going to set goals for the department, he reasoned, perhaps he should come up with some of his own.

So he did.

To start, he had to ask, *what is important?*

Results. Those were what counted; everybody said so. But results in some areas were more important than in others. In fact, some results would be *key* to making the department perform better.

In his notebook, Joe wrote down *Key Result Area.*

Increasing output would be a key result area. Didn't all bosses want more output? Joe figured that was a safe bet.

Now how would they know whether they were making any progress? Through *measurements,* of course. They would check the number of units they currently moved to Dept O, and then check the number again after they had made some changes.

How would they know if they were successful? They needed a **goal.** Joe picked a ten percent increase as a suitable goal.

Joe Mode's Notebook

To channel action, mutually establish the following:

Key Result Area
(The direction we want to go)
Example: Increase output

Measurement
(A way to know we're moving in the right direction)
Example: Number of units moved to Dept O

Goal
(Something to tell us if we're there yet)
Example: 10% increase

Joe knew there were probably a number of other worthy key result areas, each of which would have its own measurements and goals. But "increasing output" would do for a start.

Just to be on the safe side (because he knew he

might need some approvals from her later on), Joe ran this past Mary Ellen Krabofski, who was actually quite impressed.

She immediately did some digging in her files, and from way in the back of her bottom drawer, produced a list of things Normal's top management considered to be important to the company. They had come up with this list in a closed-door, off-site meeting several years ago, which nobody ever found out about.

At the tippy-top of this list were two words:

Customer Satisfaction

"I like your idea of increasing output," said Mary Ellen. "But I think you also ought to do something to help customer satisfaction, because that's important to the company."

This was a problem for Joe Mode. Customer satisfaction? How was he supposed to know what that was? Joe had never even *met* a customer.

He retreated again to his office, where he paced back and forth.

"What *do* Normal customers want?" Joe Mode asked out loud.

"They want their normalators to work when they plug them in, that's what," said Phyllis, who was passing by.

"So *don't* they work when the customers plug them in?" asked Joe Mode.

"Not always, from what I hear," said Phyllis.

Joe Mode went out and talked to people around the department. Yes, customer complaints about quality and reliability had been filtering back through the grapevine for years. Everybody knew about them. (In fact, as Joe surmised by talking to Ralph, the inability to do anything about those complaints was a big source of Sapp for people.) And the problem they had heard most about was unreliable ramadrams.

So Joe Mode reasoned that if the department increased ramadram reliability, customers might be more satisfied.

And he wrote this out.

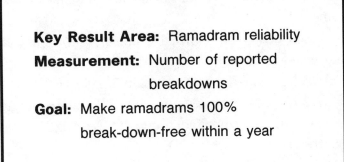

Key Result Area: Ramadram reliability
Measurement: Number of reported
breakdowns
Goal: Make ramadrams 100%
break-down-free within a year

Joe was quite pleased with the way this had worked out, because the two goals complemented each other. Finding ways to increase product reliability would mean less re-work, which would save time. And finding ways to save steps and time might help simplify the work, which would mean fewer mistakes, which would improve reliability.

Joe went back to Mary Ellen and she immediately approved his strategy. She still did not like him to hold meetings, of course, so Joe waited until a day when she was out of town. Then he got everybody together and gave them the big picture in terms they could understand.

More output, he told them, meant customers would get their normalators faster, rather than having to wait.

Higher ramadram reliability meant normalators that worked when the customers plugged them in.

Together, these results meant more satisfied customers.

Which meant the Normal Company got money in the mail.

Which meant the company could pay everyone.

Which meant everyone in Dept N would continue to have jobs and could feel proud of the work they had contributed.

"So that's what it's all about!" Joe heard someone say. "I never knew!"

Zapp!

Then Joe Mode asked for their help in finding ways to reach the goals he had set. He helped each person come up with measurable goals that would enable Dept N to reach its overall goals.

Each person had personal goals . . .

To help meet Dept N's goals . . .

To help meet the company's goals.

For the very first time, every person knew what was important, why it was important, and why *they* were important and had a place in the big picture.

That was an enormous ZAPP!!

19

*T*ime passed, and indeed performance in Dept N began to improve. One day, Joe Mode was walking down the aisle when Marty stopped him.

"How am I doing?" asked Marty.

"Uh, OK," said Joe Mode.

The next day a couple of other people asked, "Say, Joe, how's the department doing?"

"We're doing pretty good," said Joe.

After that, they soon quit asking. A few days later, Joe noticed in the measurements that everybody was slacking off. Now Joe was afraid to say anything, thinking he would only tell them if they were doing "pretty good."

Ralph had made his own measurements of the Zapp levels, and found indeed they had been falling off.

"What's going on? I told them they were doing pretty good," said Joe.

"But what does *pretty good* mean?" Ralph chided. "Joe, if you were a basketball player, how good could

116

you be if you could never see whether the ball went into the basket? Or what if you had to play every day, but no one would tell you the score? People who are involved in their work want to know exactly how they're doing and how the whole team is doing—and not tomorrow, but today."

"I see what you mean," Joe said.

By the next afternoon, there were big chalkboards placed around Dept N. On the boards were written each person's goals, the team's goals, and the department's goals. Next to these on each board was a graph of how the person, the team, and the department were progressing.

Joe taught the people how to keep track of their own performance and update their *own* charts. This gave every worker prompt feedback on how they were doing and an even stronger feeling of ownership.

As soon as people knew how well they were doing—Zapp!—the lightning level began to climb.

Despite Joe's fears, even bad news could be a Zapp. People tried a little harder if they saw they were falling behind.

And if someone continued to fall behind, Joe Mode did not have to be the "bad guy" in telling the person his or her performance was off; the measurements told the story.

But most of the time, measurements on the graphs

went up, up, up. It was not long before Dept N had reached its output goals. Joe talked to the people again, and together they came up with new goals—for themselves and for the department as a whole.

One afternoon, Joe Mode got a call from Mack, the supervisor of Dept O, which was receiving most of that increased output from Dept N.

He said, "Joe, I'd like you to come down and take a look at something."

"OK, I'll be right over," said Joe.

When he got to Dept O, Mack was waiting.

"Look at all this!" said Mack.

Indeed, there was a mountain of output from Dept N sitting in the hallway—piles and piles, and stacks and stacks of it.

"Fantastic, isn't it!" Joe Mode said proudly.

"Well, yes and no," said Mack. "See, it used to be we kept needing more and more ramadrams because out of every 50 you gave us we'd find mistakes in 25. Now that you're giving us mostly good ones, we don't need that many. On the other hand, you keep giving us more and more ramadrams, but we ran out of dooverdogs two days ago."

"Dooverdogs, huh? I'll see if we can boost our output on those," said Joe Mode.

"No, no, Joe. Right now, we don't need *more* output; we just need the *right* output at the *right time.*"

"Oh," said Joe.

He went back to Dept N. What would he do now? Everyone was Zapped into producing more and more, and better and better. Well, better and better was still all right, but more and more had to stop. Priorities had to shift. How could he get people to go in a new direction without Sapping the momentum?

First, he went out and congratulated everyone on meeting the goals for increased output and reliability.

Zapp!

Then for increased output he substituted a new key result area, measurement, and goal.

He said, "We will no longer be measuring *increases* in output. That was important last month and we met the goal. This month we're going to measure on-time delivery, and I'd like your help reaching a new goal: to deliver exactly the kind of output needed by Dept O within ten minutes of when they need it."

They set up new charts around the department and started the new measurements. Before long, with Joe doing the other things he now did—Zapp!—people began to behave in new ways. They began to think in terms of timeliness and specific need, rather than just volume.

Changing the goal changed the direction.

Joe Mode's Notebook

- Constant performance feedback relative to goals keeps the Zapp level high.

- If possible, people should manage their own feedback system.

- Changing measurements and goals Zapps people in new directions.

20

Unfortunately, the new goals required more information to be processed by Mrs. Estello, who was still making mistake after mistake with hardly a break.

Joe went over to her one day and pointed out this fact to her.

"Oh," she said. "Is *that* what that line means when it goes off the chart and down toward the floor?"

"Yes, that's what that means, Mrs. Estello," Joe Mode explained patiently. "You see, the problem is that for the department to reach our new goal, we're going to need your help in reducing the number of mistakes in the work coming from your area."

Mrs. Estello nodded vaguely and looked as if she might be thinking about an unpleasant side effect of something she'd had for lunch.

"You've been doing this job for a long time," Joe continued. "I'm sure with your experience you can think of ways you might improve your quality and efficiency."

"I can?" she asked.

"Sure you can! Just give it a try. We'll talk about it on Wednesday, and if there are things you need, let me know," said Joe Mode.

And he went away thinking that surely Mrs. Estello would respond to what he had said.

Yet two days later, Mrs. Estello was still making all kinds of blunders. On Monday, for example, a bundle of dooverdogs arrived at Dept O when they really had needed a basket of diggywigs—all because Mrs. Estello hit the wrong code key and never looked back.

Just about everything coming from her had to be done over again, and by Wednesday her performance had even fallen off somewhat rather than improved. Other people in the department were coming to Joe and complaining.

Joe went to talk to Mrs. Estello again.

"Why do you think you're making so many mistakes?" he asked.

"I don't know," she said.

"How could you be improving?"

"I don't know."

"Didn't you come up with any ideas on what we talked about?" Joe asked.

"Not yet. I didn't have time," said Mrs. Estello.

After work Joe was telling his wife, Flo Mode, what had happened.

"She's hopeless! She'll never get it! Never in a billion years!" Joe told Flo.

"Maybe you're asking too much too soon from Mrs. Estello," Flo suggested.

"But she's holding back the whole department!" Joe cried. "I should get her fired!"

"Now, now," said Flo. "Why don't you go out in the backyard, cool down, and see what the kids are up to."

Joe figured that was a good idea. When he got outside, he found their young son, Moe, and their daughter, Bo, learning how to play baseball. He watched as little Moe Mode flailed away at the ball his older sister was pitching.

After his fourth useless swing, little Moe turned and said, "Dad, I can't do it!"

"Sure you can," said Joe.

"But I don't know how!"

So Joe came down off the porch and he worked with little Moe.

First, Joe talked with little Moe to make sure he understood the object of the game. Then they talked about important details: how Moe had to keep his eye on the ball, when to swing and when not to swing, and how to choke up on the bat to get more control.

Next, Joe said, "Now watch me." And he took the bat and showed little Moe how it was done.

Then he gave the bat back to little Moe and said, "Here, you try it now."

Which little Moe did. The ball came across the rock

they were using for home plate and little Moe swung the bat—and missed.

But, being a good dad, Joe did not yell at him. He just said, "Good swing! Now try it again. You'll get the hang of it. Remember, keep your eye on the ball."

Then he had Moe practice some more—over and over again.

Finally—CRACK!—little Moe connected and sent the ball rocketing over the back hedge.

"See, you're a natural!" called Joe as his son ran for the brick which represented first base.

But, of course, little Moe was not a natural baseball player; he had succeeded because his dad had taken the time to coach him and because he had practiced. And as Joe watched proudly while little Moe ran the bases, he suddenly realized that this is what he had to do with Mrs. Estello.

He had to be a coach.

Just as he would never tell his kids, "If you don't hit the ball the first time, you're out of the family, and I'm going to put you up for adoption," it wasn't right for him to demand too much of Mrs. Estello without helping her to live up to his expectations.

The next day, Joe went over to Mrs. Estello and said, "Mrs. Estello, I'm going to work together with you on this. Maybe if we put our heads together we can figure this out. Now first let's talk about what we're trying to accomplish. . . ."

By and by, Joe Mode found there were seven basic steps to being a good coach on the job.

He would first establish the overall purpose of the task and why it was important.

Then he would explain the process to be used.

Next he would show how the task was done or have someone provide a demonstration.

Then Joe would observe while the person practiced the process.

He would provide immediate and specific feedback, and coach again or reinforce success.

Joe would express confidence in the person's ability.

And finally, they would agree on follow-up actions.

Joe Mode's Notebook

To get maximum Zapp, many people need coaching on how to do their jobs.

Coaching steps:

1. Explain purpose and importance of what you are trying to teach.

2. Explain the process to be used.

3. Show how it's done.

4. Observe while the person practices the process.

5. Provide immediate and specific feedback (coach again or reinforce success).

6. Express confidence in the person's ability to be successful.

7. Agree on follow-up actions.

Through coaching, Joe tried to keep Mrs. Estello from making mistakes in the first place. When a new project was assigned, he coached her so she would *start out* doing it correctly. Joe found that Mrs. Estello learned much faster when he coached her before the start of a project than after she had made some mistakes. That way Mrs. Estello never had a chance to learn bad habits or get frustrated by the mistakes she was making. Coaching made a new project exciting and challenging.

Zapp!

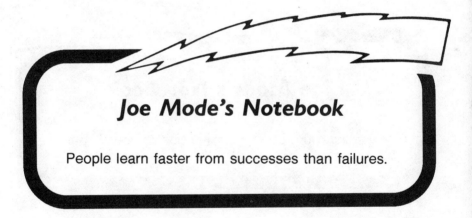

Joe Mode's Notebook

People learn faster from successes than failures.

It still took time for Mrs. Estello to improve, but she did. (In the meantime, Joe asked the other people dealing with her to come up with some ways to lighten her load, which they did.)

One of the problems was that none of the information she was processing was meaningful to her. What was a dooverdog vs. a diggywig to Mrs. Estello? She did not know that sending one rather than the other made a big difference when it got to Dept O.

Joe took her out of her work area and showed her what was what. Then he took her down to Dept O and introduced her to the employees so she could connect what they did with what she did. Little by little, Joe Mode expanded Mrs. Estello's universe.

Zapp!

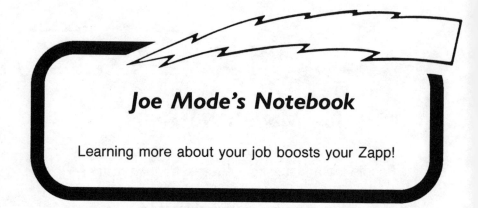

Joe Mode's Notebook

Learning more about your job boosts your Zapp!

When Mrs. Estello did something wrong, Joe tried to let the measurements tell her so. Every time Mrs. Estello did something right, Joe made sure he told her about it. He told her why it was right and talked to her about what she had to do to *keep* getting it right.

Zapp!

Still, it was not a steady climb for Mrs. Estello. From time to time, she would get angry at Joe for having her do things she didn't want to do. Or she would become defensive about her performance. Or she would get the idea that Joe was manipulating her, and her trust in him would weaken. And then she would slip back into her old ways and attitudes.

When that happened, Joe Mode relied upon the key principles he had learned to get her back on her upward path again. He did it by maintaining her self-esteem, listening and responding with empathy, asking for help in solving problems, and offering help without taking responsibility away from her.

Sure enough, Mrs. Estello would begin to improve again.

Zapp!

Joe got her some training so she could spot the problems she was having, analyze them, and come up with solutions.

Zapp!

Then Mrs. Estello *herself* asked for training to learn to use the computer better.

Zapp!

From that, she learned how to set up her keyboard so she could type a whole paragraph just by hitting one key. And she asked Joe for a program to check her spelling.

Joe Mode's Notebook

Use Key Principles to overcome blocks and slippage.

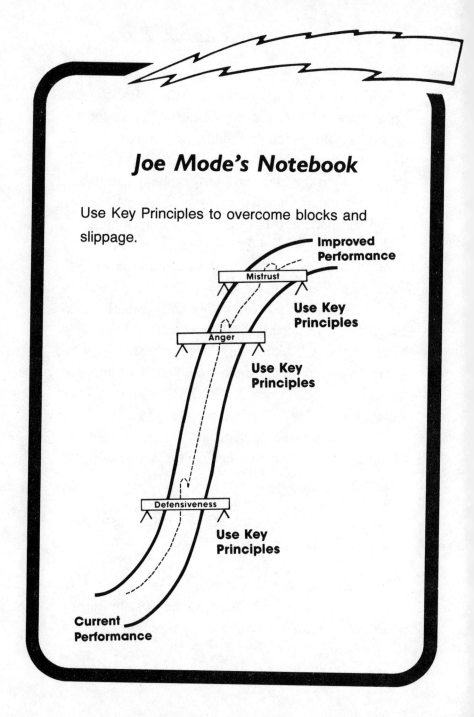

Zapp!

Then she figured out how she could type an entire form by selecting from half a dozen keys that filled in the blanks automatically.

Zapp!

And before long, Mrs. Estello was not hopeless. She was good at what she did.

She was a fully glowing member of the team.

21

By now, Joe could tell that not only was the department changing, his own job was changing as well. He was no longer the supervisor he used to be.

For years, Joe Mode had believed that he knew just about everything there was to know about supervising. In his own mind, he had seen himself as a courageous sergeant in the Army of Industry.

To be a good sergeant, he was supposed to
    Follow orders from above,
    Make all the decisions for his "platoon,"
    Keep everyone under control,
    Be hard and unapproachable,
    Bark orders at people, and
    Yell at those who did something wrong.

Hadn't that worked for John Wayne in all those war movies? Yet it no longer worked, if it ever really did, in Dept N. Something had long been missing.

What he had learned was that his job required him to be less like a tough sergeant and more like a good parent. When Joe was growing up, his parents helped him grow from a helpless kid to a responsible member of the family. Slowly they involved little Joe and his brothers and sisters in running the household. They gave them more and more responsibility and decision-making power as they grew up.

Of course, Joe knew his employees were adults and not kids, but the same ideas—growth, involvement, increasing freedom with increasing responsibility—still applied to adults in a company.

His job was no longer a matter of bossing people around. His job was to supply what people needed to grow in their work and be successful.

What did Zapped people need?

First, they needed *direction.* It was Joe's job to get people to work on the right things. He did this by establishing key result areas, goals, and measurements.

Second, they needed various types of *knowledge.* They needed job skills, technical training, information, data, understanding, expertise, and so on.

Third, they needed the company to give them the right *resources*—tools, materials, facilities, time, and money.

Fourth, they needed Joe's *support*—approval, authorization, encouragement, coaching, feedback, reinforcement, and recognition.

Instead of trying to be the solitary "hero," Joe

Mode—like Lucy Storm—was giving people whatever was required to let each of them be the "hero." He gave whatever was needed so they gave *back* their personal best.

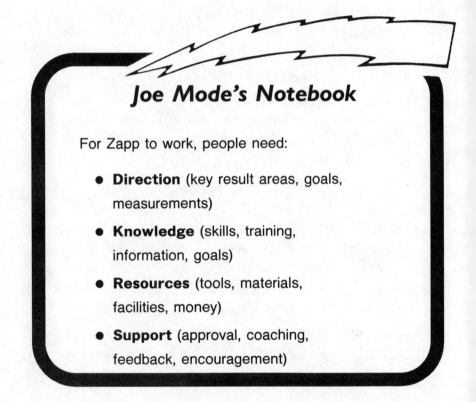

Joe Mode's Notebook

For Zapp to work, people need:

- **Direction** (key result areas, goals, measurements)
- **Knowledge** (skills, training, information, goals)
- **Resources** (tools, materials, facilities, money)
- **Support** (approval, coaching, feedback, encouragement)

All this was fine with Joe Mode. He liked his job better this way, and the people seemed to like their jobs better. Yet something was bothering him.

One evening he told Flo, "You know, I don't seem like a *supervisor* anymore. The title doesn't fit. I'm not *looking over* people."

"So what do you do in your job now?" Flo Mode asked.

"Well, I point out which direction we have to go in, and I guide them so they get there on their own, but with no one straying too far off the path, so we all get there together," said Joe.

"To me," said Flo, "that sounds like the job of a leader. You're not supervising as much as you're leading a group."

"To lead the group," Joe thought, *"rather than supervise the group."*

He sat back and tried to imagine his name linked to a new title.

Joe Mode
Group Leader

"Hmmm," he mused. "I kind of like that."

And the Zapp grew.

Joe walked through Dept N one afternoon.

He passed Marty, who told him about a problem he'd spotted, but was not a problem anymore—because he, Marty, had already solved it on his own.

Down the aisle was Luis, who was getting a group together to talk about how they could reduce errors another one-tenth of one percent, since 99.9 percent of what they produced was error free.

Then Becky went by on her way to Dept O. They had deliveries down to a five-minute leeway now, and Dept O almost always got what it needed.

Dan and Dirk were on their way to lunch. They had worked through the Normal lunch break to finish a special rush order.

And there was Mrs. Estello, master of her computer, driving that machine as fast as it would go, and having more fun than in all her other 49 years with the Normal Company put together.

Joe Mode looked around, amazed. These people were acting like owners of their work and they were proud of it. Things were not perfect, probably never would be. But a lot was better. They had a sense of who they were, and they liked it, and they knew where they were headed.

Finally, Joe got back to Ralph's work area. But Ralph was not there. A note on his door said:

**Gone to 12th
Be Back Soon**

It had been a long time since Joe had seen what all this looked like in the 12th Dimension. He suspected things would look different from what he remembered.

Having a few minutes to spare, Joe sat down in the chair by the Ralpholator. By now, Ralph had installed menu-driven software in the Ralpholator, making it easy for Joe to figure out which commands to enter.

He double-clicked the computer mouse. There was a high-pitched whine, a blinding flash, and then Joe Mode vanished.

When he opened his eyes, Joe saw Dept N in a light in which he had never seen it before. The fog had lifted. As he walked around, it was as if the sun had come out, except that the sun was inside the people.

In the shadowy corners were still some dragon eggs, and nothing could be done at the moment to dislodge them. But Joe remembered those walls of stone, glass, and steel.

Well, the stone walls were tumbling and crumbling. The glass walls had been vaporized. And the Zapp had melted holes in the steel walls, forming doors.

As Joe Mode looked around, he saw no more zombies, no more mummies, no more headless giants.

Everybody in Dept N was growing into exactly what they were—*human beings.*

Joe was happy with what he saw.

Except that Ralph was nowhere to be seen, and Joe did want to talk to him.

He decided to check if Ralph might be in Dept Z. So he left the bright lightning lights of Dept N and found his way through the still foggy corridors of the rest of the Normal Company.

He passed the mother dragon, who was wreaking havoc in the Normal Accounting Dept. and who, oddly enough, seemed a bit smaller than when he had last seen her.

He passed more dragon eggs, swarms of zombies, and lots of other strange sights. Finally, he arrived in Dept Z.

Much to his satisfaction, he saw that the Zapp of his own Dept N was now about the same as in Dept Z.

But where was Ralph? Not in Dept Z. Joe went back into the fog and checked a few more places, but Ralph was not in any of his usual haunts.

As he kept looking, Joe roamed farther and farther through the fog. Pretty soon, when he gave up and tried to go back, Joe Mode realized he was lost.

He wandered haphazardly for a while. He happened down a winding staircase, through a courtyard, and into a wide archway flanked by a massive set of gates, where a bored security guard stood leaning on his 12th Dimension spear.

On the far side of the archway, Joe Mode realized that he was *outside*. In fact, he was standing on the planks of what he came to realize was a drawbridge. When Joe turned around and looked up at the Normal

Company building as it appeared in the 12th Dimension, he saw something like a castle.

And there standing in front of him on the far side of the moat were Ralph Rosco and Lucy Storm.

"Hi, Joe," Ralph said.

"Pretty wild, isn't it?" said Lucy.

"What are you two doing here?" Joe asked.

"Ralph has been showing me around," said Lucy. "In fact, we were watching you for a while. I was even picking up a few pointers."

"You were?" asked Joe.

"I think it's time we compared notes, don't you?" asked Lucy Storm.

And they did just that.

Part 3

Super-charged Zapp!

22

As experts on the subject now agree, there are two ways to enter the 12th Dimension. The first is by sitting in the swivel chair wired to the Ralph Rosco Ralpholator. The second is to bump into someone by accident who is already *in* the 12th Dimension.

Which was what Lucy Storm had done.

Ralph had been (invisible, of course) in the 12th Dimension with Zappometer in hand as he wandered over to have a look at a new kind of lightning he had just noticed.

Lucy had been hurrying toward her desk to take a phone call—when Zapp!—she slammed right into him, was drawn into his field, and vanished from the normal world of three dimensions.

When her eyes adjusted, she'd found herself in the land of lightning bolts and strange yet brilliant visions. And here was this guy saying, "Oh, hi, remember me?

Gee, guess you'd like to know where you are and what's going on, wouldn't you?"

"Yes, please," Lucy said, hands covering her pounding heart.

So Ralph calmly reintroduced himself and gave her the grand tour. That was what they were doing when Joe Mode showed up.

Well, once she heard what had been going on, Lucy could have been a little upset that Joe Mode had not come to her and been more open about things.

But she was more interested in this new way of looking at the world, and she was even more fascinated by the power of Zapp.

"All these years I've been trying to create this, without ever knowing if it really existed," she said. "And now I can actually see it!"

"But what are you doing out *here?*" asked Joe Mode.

"It occurred to me as I was showing Lucy around," said Ralph, "that I had never seen the whole company from the perspective of the 12th Dimension. So we came out to take a look."

And they all turned toward the big, stony, dour, gray shape behind them. Actually, it was not so much like one huge castle as it was a web of smaller ones. A maze of walls, towers, and parapets. Little fortresses joined by common walls. Battlements that went up and up toward the sky, layer upon layer, much like a pyramid.

Actually, it looked a lot like the Normal organization chart. In the center, rising from the uppermost tier of the highest battlements was the tallest tower, from which flew the Normal Company flag. And there, in a balcony alcove of that tallest tower, was the president of Normal Company, Mr. Topp, who was drinking a cup of coffee as he read the latest monthly reports.

"But where is Dept N?" asked Joe Mode, who wanted to know (as Lucy had before he had arrived) where his own department stood in the scheme of things.

"It's over there. Don't you see it?" said Ralph, pointing to one of the smaller towers on the outer battlements.

Joe finally saw which tower Ralph was pointing to. It was, of course, the one with the glow of lightning bolts behind its windows.

Then Joe Mode noticed that, unlike the other towers of the company castle, which typically had narrow rectangular windows, this tower—their tower—had little *round* windows.

And *fins.*

It also had a smoother, sleeker shape than the other towers.

This tower seemed to be much more *fluid* somehow.

As Joe scanned the sight before him, there, on the far side of the outer battlements, was another tower, also with fins and little round windows behind which flickered and glowed the lightning of Zapp!

It was, of course, Dept Z.

Whatever these new towers were, they were different from the others. Something very extraordinary was taking place.

Joe could see they were no longer shapes of set stone, but shapes transforming, evolving into something new.

23

Well, they all found it very interesting to look at the company this way, but it was time to get back to work. So the three of them returned to the normal world of Normal. In parting, there were lots of promises to talk often and to keep in touch.

But those promises were never kept.

In days to come, they were all much too busy with their own departments.

Lucy Storm did come over to Dept N a couple of times and asked to use the Ralpholator so she could do some exploring on her own.

And then lots of people it seemed were coming over from Dept Z to take a trip to the 12th Dimension. Not just individuals, but *whole groups.*

This miffed Joe Mode a bit. These groups coming in and out were somewhat disruptive and they were making demands on Ralph's time.

But this was a minor irritation. Joe Mode had lots of other things to keep him occupied. Chief among them was the task of trying to keep everyone Zapped.

One afternoon on his way home, Joe finally admitted something to himself he really didn't want to.

He was finding it harder, not easier, to keep people Zapped as time went on.

He was using everything he already knew, but he could not get the kind of quantum improvement in involvement and performance he had been getting before. Zapp as he would, he even found the overall lightning level falling off just a little. And he knew it even without Ralph telling him the exact measurements.

"What else can I do?" Joe Mode asked himself as he drove home. Then he shrugged and said, "Well, maybe we've reached the limits. Maybe this is as good as it gets."

About a week later, Ralph came into Joe Mode's office with a copy of *The Normal News,* the company newspaper, and said, "Hey, Joe, have you seen this?"

On the front page was a story that read:

Dept Z Paves Way to Rewarding New Business for Normal

Normal Vice President Mary Ellen Krabofski congratulated Dept Z's Lucy Storm and a group of employees who call themselves the "Diamond Team" for developing what is expected to be a profitable new business for the Normal Company.

"The team deserves all the credit," Ms. Storm said. "Their hard work, enthusiasm, and creativity are what allowed us to develop ways to overcome the fathomless pitfalls in our path and make this new business take off."

"A whole new business? What's going on over there?" asked Joe Mode.

"I don't know," said Ralph. "I figured we knew as much as they did, so I haven't been checking on them lately."

"Fire up that machine of yours and let's go find out what they're doing," said Joe.

When they got to Dept Z, everything at first looked about the same as always. Lucy was walking around in her wizard hat and the usual miraculous things were going on. Then Ralph started getting a very strong reading on his Zappometer.

"Look at this, Joe. Dept Z is running at 100 bolts an hour!" said Ralph. "The best we've ever done is 75."

"How could that be?" asked Joe Mode. "We were the same just a little while ago."

"What can I say?" said Ralph. "The Zappometer does not lie."

Then Ralph saw that new, strange kind of lightning

he noticed the day Lucy Storm had bumped into him. It came from a group working on the far side of the bottomless chasm.

Joe and Ralph moved closer to the new lightning, and as they did, the Zappometer went off the scale.

But they didn't need an instrument to tell them they were seeing something different from the usual Zapp they were accustomed to seeing.

Because this was a *wheel* of lightning.

There was the Diamond Team working on their gem-encrusted mountain. The hot-air balloon they had first used to get across the chasm hung limply from a rocky ledge, discarded on the other side and swaying in the 12th Dimension breeze. The team now had built a bridge across the chasm.

This wheel of Zapp ran round and round between them, both directions at once, and back and forth over the diameter of the group as they worked.

The kind of Zapp that Ralph and Joe had been used to seeing in the 12th Dimension was mostly the simple, linear kind. That is, it sparked from the person in charge to the person *working* for the person in charge—from Joe to Ralph or from Joe to Mrs. Estello. It did not go round and round, from one person to the next to the next, and back and forth through the group.

But this Zapp did.

"So what is it?" Joe Mode asked.

"Gee, I don't know," said Ralph. "It must be because of the work team we read about in *The Normal News."*

"What could be enZapping about a work team?" Joe Mode wondered. "They've been tried before."

"What I want to know," said Ralph, "is what's making it happen? Lucy is way over there. She's not around to do the Zapping."

And that was the other very unusual thing about this type of Zapp. It seemed to have no single source, but instead was generated by the group itself.

Joe Mode watched the wheel of Zapp and knew there was more to Zapp than was yet known. Could Zapping people in teams be the next step?

It couldn't be too hard to set up some teams, Joe reasoned. That night, he went over the list of employees in Dept N and divided them into teams. The next day, he came to work and told everybody which teams they were on. Then he asked Ralph to monitor what happened.

A few days later, Ralph came in to announce that the Zapp count had risen. It was now up to 76 bolts per hour instead of 75.

"Is that all?" said Joe Mode. "OK, Ralph, I'd like your help finding out what's wrong with our teams."

After some investigating, Ralph determined that the teams were not really teams. The Zapp still flowed from Joe Mode to each individual, rather than around and among the people in the group.

"You might be calling them teams," said Ralph,

"but the people in them have no more sense of involvement than if they were just a bunch of men and women working next to each other. They're teams in name only."

"Then how come the teams in Dept Z are enZapping and ours are not?" Joe wondered out loud.

The phone rang.

"Because ours aren't your normal work teams," said Lucy Storm when Joe Mode answered the call. "Our teams are Zapped."

24

*H*aving a group of Zapped individuals is simply not as productive as having them enZapped as a team," continued Lucy Storm, speaking from the Ral-phone.

"Where are you?" asked Joe Mode.

"I'm in the 12th. I was just checking up on my own performance, and could see you were trying to use work teams and not getting very far," she said. "You know, we really should talk more often."

"You're right. We should," Joe agreed.

"See, Joe, it's hard to keep building Zapp on an individual level," she added. "There are limits to what you can do to enZapp one person."

"But I've set up teams and I'm hardly getting anything for my trouble," said Joe.

"Our teams are different," she said. "They're . . . well, for lack of a better term, they're **Zapp Teams**."

"So how are Zapp Teams different?" asked Joe.

"They're semi-autonomous," said Lucy.

"They're what?"

"Semi-autonomous. Basically, it means that I still point the direction and assess performance and help with things the team can't handle by itself. But other than that, the team learns to run itself."

A Zapp Team, she explained, becomes semi-auton-omous over time, gradually working with less and less supervision. Once given its mission, the team be-comes largely self-governing and carries the burden of responsibility for accomplishing its goals.

"Aha!" said Joe Mode, who, having heard this, un-derstood that Zapp Teams were another extension of the same path they had been following—which was away from Sapp and toward higher and higher Zapp!

After Lucy and he hung up, Joe went to work.

First, he asked for help from the workers in setting up the teams rather than try to impose *his* setup on them.

Zapp!

The teams they created grew out of the basic func-tions and responsibility areas of Dept N. Once they were formed, Joe Mode, as the overall leader of the department, worked with each team to establish its mission. And each individual on a team had a role in that mission.

Zapp!

Joe made sure everyone understood how each

team's mission fit with the overall mission of the department and, beyond, for the entire Normal Company.

Zapp!

He made sure each team had its own set of key result areas, measurements, and goals and that people on the team understood what those were.

Zapp!

Finally, Joe made sure that every team set up its own scoreboard to show how well it was doing.

Zapp!

From then on, when Joe asked for help in solving a big problem, he asked the team. When he offered help, he offered help to the team.

Zapp!

Day by day, the Zapp grew within the teams. They came to life. They generated a spirit of their own. And the Zapp grew within all of Dept N.

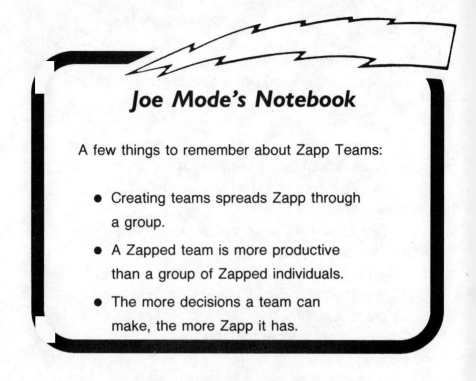

Joe Mode's Notebook

A few things to remember about Zapp Teams:

- Creating teams spreads Zapp through a group.
- A Zapped team is more productive than a group of Zapped individuals.
- The more decisions a team can make, the more Zapp it has.

Each team had a leader. Unlike Joe, the Zapp Team leader came from the ranks of the workers, from the team itself, and was not injected into the group from the outside.

The team leader was always someone who was one of the most Zapped of the group, but also one of the most enZapping to others. The leader's role was to coordinate all the things going on in the team and to help Joe nurture the group along on its mission.

Joe Mode, of course, remained the overall Group Leader, as he was now accustomed to thinking of himself.

Sometimes the people on the team could not work things out among themselves, and they would come to Joe or Joe would have to step in. But in time, Joe found that they could handle most things on their own most of the time.

They scheduled their own work.

They set priorities for team projects they had to work on.

They determined who would do what jobs.

The teams even organized vacation leave and other time off. When people called in sick, the team members either had to close ranks to get the work done themselves or arrange for someone outside the group to fill in for the person absent.

In exchange for handling all these things, Joe had to supply help in lots of new ways.

Each Zapp Team needed time and a place where they could talk things over. Even providing the place to meet was not easy. And allowing time away from actually getting the work done was always tough.

Then Joe discovered that in order for people to function as members of a team, they needed some new skills. They had to learn new "people" skills— how to interact with one another, how to work things out among themselves when egos and personalities clashed, how to hold effective meetings, how to solve problems as a group, etc.

Joe found a program that provided skills training in

a series of three-hour sessions. Scheduling was kind of tough, but once he got everyone through training, the improvement was immediate.

But they also needed new technical skills. To be able to share responsibilities, they had to know about each other's jobs and they had to be able to *do* each other's jobs.

An even bigger reason for more technical training was to enable the Zapp Teams to improve quality and productivity. To make a perfect ramadram, people on a team had to understand what could make ramadrams imperfect. This meant understanding some of the engineering and physics involved.

And of course there were always new, more powerful machines showing up in Dept N, which meant the teams needed training in how to use them.

At first, Joe Mode tried to train everyone at the same time. With the "people" skills, this worked fine. It was enZapping to have everyone sharing the same knowledge of how to interact with each other and make decisions effectively.

But with the technical skills, dumping the same training on everyone all at once often just didn't work.

For instance, it so happened that Joe knew statistical process control (SPC) to be a valuable tool in making quality improvements. So he got the approval to train Dept N in SPC.

Everybody dutifully sat through the classes. But

when they got back to their jobs, most of them didn't have the opportunity to use SPC right away. When the time finally rolled around for them to try what they had learned, people had forgotten what they were supposed to do.

There was much rolling of eyes and reddening of faces as Joe Mode went about the rather embarrassing job of having to *re*train people.

After that, Joe learned to hold off training until a person or a team encountered a situation where they really *needed* to learn more—until "the teachable moment" as the Normal corporate training manager called it. Then people would learn more quickly, apply what they learned more effectively, and remember it better.

Joe Mode often had to go to Mary Ellen Krabofski for the resources his teams needed. As Mary Ellen was not the most receptive boss in the world in those days, sometimes she would approve his requests with a handshake and a smile; other times she would give him a cranky and gruff rebuff.

But as Joe Mode's dad used to say, "Where there's a will, there's a way." And Joe had the will, and each time he found a way to get what his teams needed.

Joe Mode's Notebook

A few things that boost the voltage of Zapp Teams:

● Give the team a say in who works on the team.

● Establish a mission for the team.

● Provide time and places for the team to meet.

● Provide technical training at "the teachable moment."

● Provide "people" skills for interacting, solving problems, making decisions, and taking action.

People working in the Zapp Teams began to get involved in new kinds of decisions. They helped decide who would work with whom, who would do what, what had to be done, how soon it had to be done, etc.

Their responsibilities expanded. But their responsibilities were also shared by the group. Each person had partners to count on.

Not all of these new responsibilities were entirely pleasant. It became the team's responsibility for the work to get done on time and to pull together when problems arose. If somebody goofed off, it meant everybody else had to work harder to get the job done.

Now to most people, these kinds of things were not so nice. But they were more than offset by lots of things just about everybody really liked.

For instance . . .

They liked having a voice.

They liked agreeing on what to do rather than being told what to do.

They liked the variety of switching jobs within the team and the flexibility of trading for easier jobs on days when their energy was low and for tougher jobs when they got bored and craved more Zapp.

They liked the sense of purpose in having a group mission and being part of the journey to the goal.

They liked being on the inside.

They liked having control over problems.

They liked working with no one looking over their shoulders.

They liked sharing ideas.

They liked sharing the success of the team.

They liked sharing in the power of the team to get things done.

All of these things were very satisfying. And that was why the Zapp Teams worked.

Joe Mode's Notebook

Zapp Teams can take lots of responsibility.

For instance, they might . . .

- Determine who works on what.
- Handle absenteeism and performance issues.
- Get involved in all aspects of their work.
- Select their own team leader from their ranks.
- Find opportunities to improve quality and productivity (and work to realize those opportunities).
- Perform basic maintenance.
- Schedule vacations.

Part 4

The Zapped Company

25

So, you might ask, what was all this looking like now from the perspective of the wild and weird 12th Dimension?

It was dazzling.

Absolutely da-ZZ-ling.

Before the Teams, each person in Dept N had been a glowing island of Zapp. Now the islands were joined, and the flow of Zapp had become wheels, and the wheels were revving freely.

Ralph even had to change the scale on the Zappometer to account for Zapp Teams.

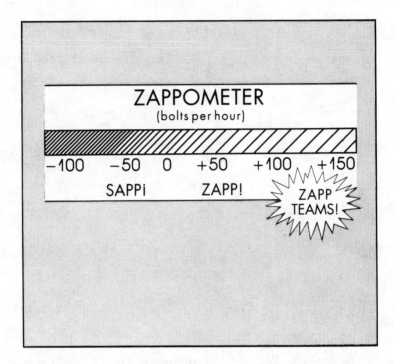

But seen from the outside . . .

Well, one day Joe, Lucy, and Ralph were outside in the 12th Dimension taking a look at the Normal castle and the effect of the wheels of lightning from the Zapp Teams.

Indeed, the towers of Dept N and Dept Z were less castle-like than ever. They even appeared to be trying to take off.

"You know," said Joe Mode, "they kind of look like . . . well, like they could go and do just about anything."

"They're like starships, Joe," said Ralph.

"Starships?"

"Sure, ready to take off on a mission."

Well, they may have had the makings of a pair of 12th Dimension starships, but these amazing vehicles were being held on the ground, very much attached to the gray, heavy mass of the rest of the Normal castle, unable to do what they were capable of doing.

Yet, this seemed to be an appropriate *new* challenge—to somehow make the starships fly.

To do it, they would need all the Zapp they could get. But Ralph (and everyone else as well) had noticed that just when a wheel of Zapp was turning its fastest and shining its brightest, some source of Sapp would come along to dull it down.

Some of these Sapps were BIG ONES.

Big enough even to brake the wheels almost to a stop.

For instance . . .

One morning, Hugh Galahad (wearing a normal business suit instead of his 12th Dimension shining armor) came into Dept N with some technicians and announced that a totally new set of equipment was to be installed.

And Hugh, without explaining anything to anybody, had the Normal technicians go to work. Within hours, Dept N had a new system that nobody knew anything about.

"What makes this equipment better than what we had before?" Becky asked.

Well, Galahad wouldn't even talk to her. But one of the technicians finally answered her. "It's pretty technical," he said. "You wouldn't understand. All you have to know is that you press the blue button when the green light comes on. If the red light comes on, call us. We'll take care of everything."

Sappi

Later that day in Dept Z, Lucy Storm was coming back from lunch when she was greeted by a man in a white lab coat.

"Good afternoon. I'm O. MacDonald, E.I.E.I.O.," he said.

They shook hands.

"Tell me, what does E.I.E.I.O. stand for?" asked Lucy.

"Effective Industrial Engineering Interdepartmental Observer," said MacDonald.

"Well, Mr. MacDonald, what can I do for you?"

"I'm here to do time studies so that efficiency may be improved," said O. MacDonald, holding up his stopwatch.

Knowing the way Normal did its time studies, Lucy knew this would be a Sapp on the department. She tried to explain about the teams and getting people involved. She knew there were enZapping ways for an industrial engineer to get the job done. But O. Mac-Donald was set in his ways, and he had his orders from on high. He set to work and there was nothing Lucy could do about it.

O. MacDonald treated the workers objectively. That is, like objects. He stood there with his stop-watch, recorded the measurements, and did not in-volve the person doing the work. Later, O. Mac-Donald imparted to the workers the fruit of his scientific study.

"Now don't reach over there," said O. MacDonald, E.I.E.I.O. "Always reach over here. And don't bend this way; bend that way."

Sappi

And then there was management.

Mary Ellen Krabofski had not had a moment's peace for months.

You see, by now, the mother dragon's eggs were beginning to hatch. And the first thing those baby dragons did was to gorge themselves on anything that could fire up their huffer-puffers.

This actually was not much of a problem for the Zapp Teams. Against the united Zapp of a team, the dragons had no chance. The Zapp Teams, by working steadily to improve quality and overall performance, gave them no food. And the dragons could not grow.

But in some of the other departments, it was a different story. Some of those baby dragons got very big very quickly.

Which was why Mary Ellen had no peace. She was still behind the wheel of the executive fire truck. With all these little fires from the baby dragons breaking out, she was racing here and racing there and wondering why no one could handle problems like she could.

Finally, she had had enough. She went right to Mr. Topp and the management committee and made a presentation showing that she desperately needed more staff.

After clearing his throat many times and exchanging glances with the rest of the committee, Mr. Topp reluctantly took out his pen and signed the authorization.

Outside in the 12th Dimension, a new layer of battlements went up on the castle.

The tallest tower got even taller and the castle got heavier. But the really bad news was that the other towers below got covered up.

Joe Mode was on his way to see Mary Ellen Krabofski about some things needed in Dept N when he was intercepted by a man in the hallway to her office.

"Hello, I'm Biff Buffer, the new assistant executive

to the vice president," he said. "Talk to me when you need anything from now on."

Joe Mode made his request, and Biff said, "Hmmm. Well, I can't give you the go-ahead on something like that right now. I'll have to clear that with M.E. next time I see her, and of course we'll have to check with the new deputy senior assistant to the vice president and the new task force committee. Check back with me in about three or four weeks and maybe we'll have had some word by then."

"Three or four weeks?" asked Joe Mode.

"Weeks? Did I say *weeks?* Oh, sorry. I meant three or four *months.*"

Sappi

Down in Dept C, where they dealt with Normal customers all day long, it was not unusual to encounter a normalator buyer who had a special problem or needed extra attention. And yet, Normal Company policy often made it next to impossible for the people in Dept C to take care of the customer's needs.

One typical afternoon, a customer came in, sat down with the Normal service representative, and said, "I'm having some trouble with the normalator I bought a couple months ago. It makes a noise like a bunch of kids scratching their fingernails on a blackboard, vibrates so much it waddles across the floor, and gives off a terrible odor."

"Gee," said the Dept C service rep, who had very little training either in normalators or customers, "I don't know what to tell you. Maybe it's designed to be like that."

"I don't think so," said the customer.

"Well, I'll see if I can find it in the manual," said the service rep.

Half an hour later, with the customer impatiently squirming in her chair, the service rep said, "Oh, here's what must be wrong. You need the Anti-hyper-normalating Reverse Attachment."

"Oh," said the customer. "Good. I'll take one."

"Sorry. That's only available on the Model-1 Deluxe," said the service rep, "and I see you have a Model-2 Stripped."

"But the salesperson said your company could take care of all my normalator needs," said the customer. "Why can't you take mine back and give me a trade-in on the one I need?"

"I'm not allowed to do that," said the service rep.

"Well, then, I want my money back!" said the customer.

"I'm sorry, but company policy is not to accept any normalator for return after the 30-day warranty period."

"Then what *can* you do?!" demanded the customer.

"Not much," thought the service rep.
Sappi

All of these Sapps came from forces outside the departments where the people felt their impact. There was little Joe Mode or Lucy Storm or any other department head could do about them.

But Joe and Lucy did ask for help from Ralph, who performed a study of all the factors from outside a department that could Zapp or Sapp.

This was what Ralph found:

First, that the group leader or supervisor had the most power to Zapp or Sapp a person on the job.

After the person's immediate boss, other people *around* the worker had the greatest influence on Zapp.

These people included co-workers, technical staff, and maintenance and support personnel.

Next most influential in enZapping or Sapping was the organization itself, including its structure, policies, and systems—payroll, benefits, suggestion systems, and so on.

In the same league as the organization was the union (for those who *were* unionized or had to deal with the union).

Despite their varying influences, all of these had an effect.

Joe Mode's Notebook

Who determines how Zapped (or Sapped) an
employee is?

In order of importance:

1. The person's immediate boss (the
   group leader)

2. The other people who affect the
   person's job (suppliers, services,
   support)

3. Higher management

4. The organization and its systems

By far, the most important enZapping
influence is the supervisor or manager
to whom the employee directly reports.

"Joe, the plain truth is that there are lots of things affecting Sapp and Zapp that we can't control," said Lucy.

"Well, we're still better off than we were," said Joe Mode. "My life is easier. I'm not about to go back to Sapping people. Everybody in the department is happier."

"True, but I'm not satisfied with that," said Lucy. "I think it's time to talk to Mary Ellen."

26

*T*hough she could be quite trollish from time to time, Mary Ellen Krabofski was no dummy. In fact, she was very smart. She soon began to notice that she had to spend very little time in either Dept N or Dept Z solving problems.

Of course, she knew about some amazing things going on in those departments, such as the new business the Diamond Team had opened, and she especially wanted to know why Joe Mode's Dept N, whose performance had always been mediocre at best, was now so good.

In fact, word was spreading quickly throughout the Normal Company. Lots of people wanted to transfer into either Dept N or Dept Z because both had earned the reputation of being great places to work. Even some of the other supervisors had begun to ask what was going so *right* in Dept N and Dept Z.

It was about then that Joe Mode and Lucy Storm came to the same conclusion. It was time to take the wraps off, time to go public. They had done in their own departments as much as they could with Zapp. To go further, they needed the help of the organization at large.

Joe and Lucy went to the Zapp Teams and asked for their help in developing a presentation for management. And the teams went to work. They set up a presentation date with Mary Ellen, who was quite receptive to hear what they had to say. As the big day approached, Joe and Lucy coached the Zapp Team presenters on what to expect, what would be expected of them, and how to make a successful presentation.

The date arrived. Joe Mode opened the presentation. He began by giving a glowing description of the power of Zapp and how fantastic it was. Of course, no superlative was too great for his description.

Then he said, "Mary Ellen, we've wired your chair to the Ralpholator. We're going to turn it on now, and in a moment you'll be whisked to the 12th Dimension and have a chance to see the wonders of Zapp at work right before your very eyes."

Then he turned to the curtain behind him and said, "OK, hit it Ralph."

There was a high-pitched whine. Followed by a low-pitched whine. And nothing happened.

"Excuse me. We seem to be having some technical difficulties," said Joe.

Ralph's grimy face appeared from behind the curtain.

"Bad news, Joe. The Ralpholator is busted. It blew its dooverdogs."

Joe Mode turned and looked at Mary Ellen Krabofski.

The somewhat cross-eyed expression on her face said it all:

Lightning, huh? Human lightning you say? Yeah, right. *Wheels* of lightning no less. Sure. Was there a *truck* attached to the wheels? Did you happen to get its license number?

Who could believe such nonsense?!

Well, Joe Mode made a smart decision. He had them continue with the presentation. The Zapp Teams came on one by one. They talked about the measurements. They showed where they had been, where they were now, and where they wanted to go. They talked about quality, productivity, expanding businesses, new businesses, lower costs, higher income, customer satisfaction, all the things that are magical music to a manager's ears.

And the *way* the Zapp Teams talked demonstrated that Normal employees could take responsibility for their work on an everyday basis to a degree that people like Mary Ellen never would have thought possible.

As it turned out, they didn't need the Ralpholator or the 12th Dimension to convince Mary Ellen Krabofski. By the end of the presentations, she was positively Zapped!

Most of all, she wanted her other departments to be Zapped the same way.

"We have to tell everyone about this!" said Mary Ellen. She was very excited. "I want every supervisor—err, what are you calling yourselves? Group leaders? That's it, *group leaders!* I want every one of them to start using Zapp ASAP!!"

No one is more dedicated to a cause than a skeptic who becomes convinced.

First, she scheduled a big meeting of all the supervisors, attempting to convince them that Zapp is the way to go for everybody.

This didn't work.

The other supervisors nodded their heads, agreed that Zapp made sense, and then went back to being the supervisors they had always been.

But from this, Mary Ellen learned something important.

To create Zapp, she had to use Zapp.

The other departments had to discover Zapp on their own. With her enZapping help, of course.

She began with the first three steps to Zapp.

1. **Maintain self-esteem.**
2. **Listen and respond with empathy.**
3. **Ask for help in solving problems.**

She started practicing them in all her dealings with people, for the steps were as applicable to her as they were to Joe Mode, Lucy Storm, or anyone else in a leadership role.

Then she applied the soul of Zapp:

Offer help without taking responsibility.

But, as a manager, she had another very essential role to play: to support the kind of environment where Zapp could develop and flourish.

For instance, she encouraged all her managers and supervisors to get formal training in Zapp and made available the resources for this to take place.

Then, for all departments, just as Joe Mode had done for Dept N, Mary Ellen had the supervisors develop performance guidelines with key result areas, measurements, and goals.

But one of the most important things Mary Ellen had to do as a manager was protect people from the Sapping things that the company might attempt to put upon them and to encourage the Zapping things the company could offer.

Joe Mode's Notebook

Management's role in spreading Zapp:

1. To protect people from the Sapping things that the company might attempt to put upon them while supporting and encouraging the Zapping things the company can offer.
2. To be sure that subordinate managers have the skills required to Zapp (and if they don't, get them into training).
3. To model Zapp.
4. To coach subordinate managers in how to use and improve their Zapp skills.
5. To reward performance resulting from Zapp.

Overall: to create an environment where Zapp can happen.

To be quite honest, it took Mary Ellen a long time to relinquish the keys to the executive fire truck. But as she continued to apply Zapp, a change came over her.

When Joe Mode took his occasional walks around the 12th Dimension, he hardly recognized Mary Ellen Krabofski. Her color was not ghastly green any longer. Her scales had melted. Her tail grew shorter, and disappeared. Soon, she was no longer a troll. Zapp had changed her into a human being, the true form of all good managers.

27

Biff Buffer was as nervous as a 40-year-old quarterback holding out for a fatter contract on the day when the final cuts are made.

As a middle manager, Biff knew his job security was a sure thing no more. The Normal Company, like many, had been looking to trim middle management positions for a long time simply to reduce costs. Now it turned out that this also was enZapping to the organization.

Time after time, new layers of management produced round after round of Sapp. When layers of management were stripped away, there was a big increase in Zapp. Without Biff Buffer and others like him, the Zapp that higher management had always enjoyed could reach more of the people the top managers were managing.

When Mary Ellen Krabofski called Biff into her

office one Friday, Biff imagined he heard the upswing of the ax.

But Mary Ellen had something much smarter in mind.

"Biff, you're an intelligent and capable manager. It's the nature of your position that's the issue, not your professional performance," said Mary Ellen, attempting to maintain Biff's self-esteem.

"Well, I can always try to work harder and be much more efficient, if you'll just give me the chance," said Biff.

"I sense that you're nervous about your job, and I'd like to put your mind at ease," she said, responding with empathy after having listened to what Biff had (and had not) said.

Then she asked for help in solving a problem, saying, "In fact, I'd like your help in an important undertaking. With the advancement of Zapp, and with increases in productivity, we're going to have a number of talented people in Normal with less and less to do. I'd like you to help me find new challenges for them. I'd like you to put together one of the Zapp Teams that will develop new businesses into which we can shift under-utilized people and which can generate more income for the company."

Biff Buffer sat bolt upright in his chair. He was feeling the fear of the new challenge and the excitement of working to meet it.

Mary Ellen then gave Biff some general direction on what kinds of businesses he should think about so that later he wouldn't Sapp himself on the overwhelming realm of possibilities to consider.

Then she said, "I'd like for us to meet again after you've had time to put together some ideas," and offered to help without taking responsibility. "Talk to me whenever you need to about resources you'll have to have to get this done."

Zapp!

Biff Buffer caught the lightning Mary Ellen Krabofski had thrown him and he ran with it.

Within a week, he had a Zapp Team composed of other middle managers and staff people. They went to work on ways to expand the Normal Company *outward* toward new horizons (rather than *upward,* which made the Normal Company top-heavy).

That is, instead of being overhead to the company, they built revenues. Instead of checking up on people and creating rules to try to control everybody, they were inventing new businesses of their own to manage.

This made the managers (and everybody else) a lot happier, and made the Normal Company a lot more profitable.

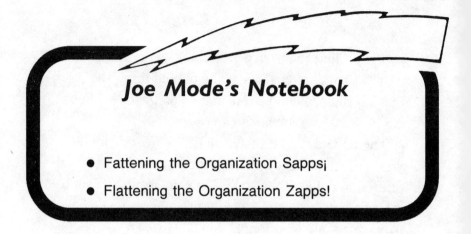

Joe Mode's Notebook

- Fattening the Organization Sapps¡
- Flattening the Organization Zapps!

The Diamond Team was hauling in business by the ton for Normal. The work load had grown so much that they couldn't possibly get everything done. They just plain needed more people.

As she was obliged by Normal policy to do, Lucy Storm went to the Personnel Dept. with the proper authorizations, and the Personnel Dept. put her hiring request in their in-basket.

A while later, Floyd showed up.

"They sent me down. Guess I'm supposed to work here or something," said Floyd.

Lucy introduced him to the Diamond Team. And the team took an instant disinterest in Floyd.

It wasn't that there was anything *wrong* with Floyd. He was not wanted by the police and he had all the proper technical qualifications for the job. But nobody could get very excited about having Floyd around.

Why should they? No one on the Diamond Team had been involved in picking Floyd. Nothing was personally at stake for any of them if Floyd didn't work out.

Not even Lucy Storm had a stake in Floyd's success. Nobody had asked her if it was OK to send Floyd down to work in Dept Z.

And Floyd was not very excited about Dept Z. And the Diamond Team? Big deal. They hadn't hired him. The *Personnel Dept.* had hired him. Floyd secretly harbored great affection for the Personnel Dept.

Floyd was Sapped for a long time.

Lucy knew this was so, and the next time the Diamond Team needed a new employee, she asked Mary Ellen to talk to the Personnel Dept. about modifying their procedures to make them more en-Zapping.

So Mary Ellen presented the problem to Personnel and asked for their help in working with Lucy and other group leaders to solve it.

The next time Dept Z needed a new employee, the results were very different.

The Zapp Team actually selected the person they wanted to work with.

The Personnel Dept. acted more as a teacher and consultant in the process so that the team would make a good choice. It also had a controlling role to make sure laws were obeyed and compensation standards were observed.

But the team actually did the hiring.

This was a big Zapp for everyone.

It was a Zapp for the Personnel Dept. because they had a new professional challenge to respond to and because they knew the groups they served were getting the people they really wanted.

It was a Zapp for the team because people now had a say in who would work with them, as well as the responsibility to do everything they could to ensure that the person they picked would be successful. For the same reasons, it was a Zapp for Lucy Storm.

And it was a Zapp for the new employee, being chosen by the team and not imposed upon them. In fact, the new employee worked all the harder so as not to let Lucy or the team down.

Down in Dept C, things began to change, too.

The people in Dept C got the training they needed to know more about both Normal products and how to handle Normal customers. Then the department changed its policies to give the service representatives more leeway to do things that would satisfy the customer. Believe it or not, the service reps in Dept

C began to look forward to handling angry customers just for the challenge of making them happy.

One afternoon, a customer came in screeching, "I demand to talk to the manager! This stupid normalator makes noise like fingernails on a blackboard—!"

"And it vibrates too much and smells bad?" asked the service rep.

"That's right!" yelled the customer. "It's driving me crazy!"

"I know exactly how you feel. It's very irritating when that happens," said the rep sympathetically. "What you need is an Anti-hypernormalating Reverse Attachment. All our new models have it, but you must have one of the older ones."

"How should I know?! This is what the salesperson sold me!" said the customer.

"Tell you what I'll do," said the rep. "You give me your old model and I'll give you a new model at no extra charge."

"Oh," said the customer. "Well, I guess that would be OK."

"Give me your address and I'll have it delivered," said the rep.

"But I'd really prefer to take it with me," said the customer.

"No problem. You go get your car and I'll get a new model out of stock and bring it right out to the curb for you."

"Well, all right. Thanks!"

And the customer actually smiled.

Zapp!

Through the grapevine, Ralph Rosco had heard that Biff Buffer and his team were looking for ideas that could become the basis of new businesses for Normal.

And Ralph thought, *"Gee, I wonder if they'd be interested in my Ralpholator as a new business?"*

So he went to Joe Mode and reminded him of the promise long ago to help develop his invention. True to his word, Joe Mode did help, and he cleared the way for Ralph to go talk to Biff.

Well, Biff still had a rather bureaucratic mind, and he told Ralph to submit his idea through the Normal Suggestion System.

Ralph went back to his work area, dusted off his Normal employee handbook, and turned to the page that explained the Normal Suggestion System Procedures.

First, according to the handbook, Ralph was supposed to write down his idea on Form #1212-S and drop it in the box by the Normal cafeteria.

Next, Ralph was supposed to do nothing. He had to wait for the verdict.

In a few months, the powers that be would pass

judgment. If *they* thought the idea had merit, a check would be sent to Ralph for whatever *they* thought the idea might be worth.

From experience, Ralph could tell this was a very Sappy system. After Ralph had submitted the idea, he would soon be disinvolved. The company would own the idea.

Every idea is a mere fantasy until it is made to work. Only then is it really worth something. And because the company was buying an idea rather than something of proven value, it was hard to determine its real value.

Because Ralph was excluded from the evaluation process, he would likely have the suspicion that no matter what he was paid, the idea was really worth more than what he got.

So Ralph explained this to Joe Mode and said, "There has to be a better way."

Together they went to Mary Ellen with the suggestion that they develop a more enZapping suggestion system.

First of all, Joe had to get Ralph to take responsibility for the consequences (whether good or bad) of what he was suggesting. He had to get Ralph to examine his own idea in a practical context.

"Your Ralpholator is a neat machine, but how is the company going to make money with it?" Joe Mode asked.

Well, Ralph hadn't thought about that. "Gee, I don't know. But it must have a *zillion* applications."

"Name two," said Joe Mode.

Ralph couldn't.

"Why don't you work on that a little more and then we'll talk again," said Joe Mode.

So Ralph did some more thinking.

He reasoned that a prime market for the Ralpholator might be the mental health profession. Psychiatrists who previously could only talk to patients about their delusions could now go to the 12th Dimension and see for themselves.

With its ability to make people invisible, the Ralpholator was sure to interest the Department of Defense. Then there were the tourism and recreation industries. Jaded travelers who had been everywhere from Tokyo to Tierra del Fuego could now go to the 12th Dimension. And what amusement park would be complete without a Ralpholator?

"That's good," said Joe Mode when Ralph laid out the potential in their next meeting. "I'll clear the way for you to talk to some people in the Marketing Dept., and you can work with them to put together a marketing plan."

That was what they did.

Next, Joe helped Ralph to see that there were some annoying bugs in the design, and then got him some help from the Normal physicists in the R&D Dept.

Then Ralph went to the head of manufacturing and worked on some estimates of production costs.

Finally, Joe Mode got Ralph some basic training in how to make a business presentation.

Then *Ralph* took his idea to Biff Buffer and the new business Zapp Team. And Ralph had a lot more than just a neat machine to show them. He had a complete business plan with hard, believable numbers, a marketing strategy, and everything else he needed to convince management of the Ralpholator's true value.

Biff Buffer and the Zapp Team were so impressed that they asked Ralph to make the same presentation to Mr. Topp and the Normal management committee.

And that was how the Ralpholator got on the road to success. And that was the same suggestion system Joe Mode (and the rest of the company eventually) used for developing all kinds of improvements, from new businesses to better diggywigs.

28

Years passed.

One morning, Joe Mode was working in his office when Phyllis knocked on his door and said, "Excuse me, Joe, but there's a young man out here who says he'd like to ask you some questions about how we run the department."

Joe told her to send him in.

"What's your name?" Joe asked the young man as he sat down.

"Call me Dave," said the young man.

"Well, Dave, what can I do for you?"

"I just joined the Normal Company, and I've heard your department was one of the first to start using something called Zapp," he said.

"That's true," said Joe.

"And I've heard Zapp is the energy that enables continuous improvement."

"That's also true," said Joe.

"Well, how does it work?" asked Dave.

By now, Joe Mode was quite accustomed to inquiries by the curious. So he took Dave for a tour, showing him Dept N and introducing him to some of the Zapp Teams, whose members gladly explained what they did and how they worked together. At the end of the tour, Joe took Dave to the 12th Dimension so he could see Zapp in living color.

Finally, to give Dave the "big picture," Joe brought him to a new feature of the 12th Dimension corporate architecture. It was a big, round observation deck which afforded a magnificent view of the Normal Company and the vast business landscape surrounding it.

From horizon to horizon, through the gaps in the drifting mists and fog, they could see scattered about the countryside all kinds of company castles.

Over here, on a rocky rise, was a typical, big castle, which looked much like the Normal castle had years ago, with sentries posted and lots of people coming and going through its gates.

And over there was a crumbling, dark, deserted castle sinking into a swamp.

Off on the horizon was Stupendous, Inc., a huge, high, and impossibly complex castle with towers reaching into the clouds—into and *above* the clouds, in fact. Its top managers probably couldn't even see the ground from up there. With its miles of maze-like walls and moats, it would seem as though nothing could ever topple Stupendous, that it would stand forever.

And, yet, gliding among the tallest towers were *flying* dragons. Even as they watched, one of the dragons, clinging to the sides of one of the biggest towers, munched its way through the walls—chomp, chomp, chomp—until the tower fell over like an axed tree and landed with an enormous crash.

Indeed, for all its size and grim complexity, the Stupendous castle seemed hopelessly antiquated compared to the shape of their own Normal Company. Most of Normal these days did not even look like a castle. It looked more like a launching pad, a home base for people who, each morning, took off in a wide ranging fleet of amazing craft designed with the help of those who flew them, and each liftoff propelled by the energy of Zapp.

And as Joe and Dave looked around, they could see them out there in the wild blue, flying their missions, getting the job done.

Of course, in reality, everybody was down here on Planet Earth in good old Normalburg, USA. But, to each Normal employee, that was how it now *felt* to go to work. Their ordinary jobs were far from ordinary any more.

"Looks like we're way ahead of lots of other companies out there," said Dave.

"Yes, we are. And we're pulling away," Joe said.

"But don't we ever have trouble with dragons here?" asked Dave.

"Sure, we still have a few, and every once in a while a new one will hatch," admitted Joe. "Dragons are tough and some of them nearly immortal. But the Zapp Teams keep improving our quality and performance. Our dragons keep getting smaller and smaller, because they have less and less to feed on, as we keep getting better and better."

Joe pointed out to Dave that he should not get the idea that the transformation of Normal was finished or ever would be. For Zapp was not fixed or absolute, but a developing force for a continuous journey.

Off to the sides were many parts of the old castle still being remodeled, recycled into flightworthy *Zappcraft*. Even the craft now flying might evolve into new forms as time went on. And over on the next hill was the landing base for a whole new 12th Dimension fleet—the Ultranormal Division, which was expanding into fresh businesses to take the place of those becoming obsolete.

That new fleet, by the way, was commanded by none other than Biff Buffer, and managed and operated by many of those who would otherwise have been squeezed in the flattening of the Normal Company. Now they were off the ground and Zapped on a mission of their own. And Ralph was flying with them.

The Ralpholator had become a hot product and

was selling big. Ralph had outgrown his job in Dept N and was leading the product team responsible for it. With gainsharing, Ralph had made his fair share of money from his original idea, but also had the satisfaction of developing it, and now he was very loyal to the company.

All of this had taken a long time, Joe explained. It had not been easy, but it certainly had been worth it.

As they started back, Dave asked, "So Zapp is something I could use in my own job? What would I do first?"

Joe was ready for these questions because in the years since he and Ralph had first learned about Zapp from Lucy Storm, lots of people had asked him how they might generate some human lightning of their own.

"Allow me to recommend my Three-step Action Plan for Zapp Rookies," said Joe Mode.

"I won't need a Ralpholator for it, will I?" asked Dave. "I mean they're still pretty expensive."

"No, you won't need one of those," said Joe. "Let's go back to my office and I'll get you started."

The first thing Joe did when they got back was give Dave a copy of the Joe Mode Notebook so he could study the basic principles of Zapp.

"Here, read it. That's Step One. I even re-read the notebook myself every so often to refresh my memory," said Joe.

"OK, but is reading this going to be enough?" Dave asked.

"Probably not," said Joe. "That's why I suggest you try Step Two. Come with me."

And he took Dave down the hall to introduce him to the special Zapp section of Normal's training department.

"Dave, meet Lucy Storm," said Joe Mode. "She's now the head of this section."

"Pleased to meet you, Dave," said Lucy. "Are you here to get some Zapp training?"

"Gee, I don't know. Do I have to?" asked Dave.

"Well, you might learn the skills to improve Zapp by trial and error, the way I did," said Joe. "But that takes a long time and you can make lots of unnecessary mistakes. What I recommend is that you build your skills in one of Lucy's training programs so you're more likely to succeed with Zapp the first time you try."

Dave considered that. "Yes, that does sound more efficient."

"And it'll be easier on the old anxiety level," added Joe.

With that, Dave signed up for Lucy's introductory program.

Then as he and Joe were leaving, Dave asked, "And what's the third step?"

"Don't stop," said Joe.

"What do you mean by that?"

"I mean once you're on the right path, keep trying, keep learning, keep improving, keep growing," said Joe Mode. "Or, in short, don't stop."

"Well, OK. I'll give it my best," said Dave.

"Good. And if I can be of any more help to you, let me know," said Joe.

"Thanks," said Dave as they shook hands.

And as Dave walked away, Joe Mode could almost see the Zapp beginning to grow inside a new person.

**Joe Mode's
Three-step Action Plan
for Zapp Rookies:**

1. Read (and re-read)
   the notebook!

2. Get training
   in Zapp!

3. Don't stop!
   Keep learning!

Acknowledgments

Jeff Cox, who helped me write this book, is responsible for most of the imaginative presentations of the concepts and information. His creativity and hard work in writing and editing made the book possible.

Many people from Development Dimensions International also have made substantial contributions to this book by providing content, ideas, and critiques of various manuscript drafts.

Individuals who deserve special recognition are (in alphabetical order) Ric Anthony, Linn Coffman, David Cohen, Michel Couture, Richard Davis, Anthony Del Prete, Debra Dinnocenzo, Susan Gladis, John Hayden, Mary Jenness, Anne Maers, Tim Mooney, Mike Moore, Dennis Ragan, Bob Rogers, Mary Jo Sonntag, Cheryl Soukup, Debra Walker, Rich Wellins, Laura White, and Stacy Rae Zappi.